creative amateur photography

David Kilpatrick

The author would like to thank the following for their assistance – sometimes unknowing – in the production of this book:

Dick Bryant, Osaka, Japan; Daphne Llewellyn Davies; Bill Christie; Bob Dove at KJP; Paul Davies at Paterson Products Limited; Jack Schofield; Rick Kutani; Eva Beagan at Ilford Photo; Stuart Fletcher of J. E. C. Potter & Son Ltd; Parry Williams at DRP Studios Ltd; Mike Mawer, RTS Print; Andreas Vogt; Richard Bradbury; Adrian Bassett; Andrew, Chris and Karel at Newnes Books; and Shirley.

The many members of the Minolta Club of Great Britain, and the professional contributors to Minolta Image magazine, whose bylines appear with their photographic contributions throughout the book.

Our models in various photographs – Sally Render, Tracie McGee, Cindy Milo, Anne-Marie, Maxine and Nina in Tunisia, John Gordon and all others who appear in pictures.

The line drawings throughout the book were produced by Mei Lim.

One of the almost unique aspects of this book is that nearly all the pictures, including hundreds of top quality colour illustrations, have been taken by amateurs. A small amount of professional 35mm photography has been included, but even this has been taken using very straightforward equipment and techniques.

The publishers thank Minolta (UK) Limited and the Minolta Club of Great Britain, 12, Ollerton Road, Tuxford, Nottinghamshire, NG22 0LF for their co-operation in giving access to these photographs, which are seen here for the first time outside the Club itself.

Further examples of Minolta photography can be seen quarterly in the Club's magazine.

This edition published exclusively for W.H. Smith
by
Newnes Books, 84–88 The Centre, Feltham,
Middlesex

ISBN 0 600 35858 5
Printed in Italy

CONTENTS

Introduction 8
Understanding photography 9–17
The subject 10
The eye vs. the camera 14
The camera 18–33
Light and film 19
Exposure and focusing 22
Exposure metering 28
Equipment 34–52
Choosing a camera 35
Understanding lenses 40
Accessories 50
Taking pictures 53–131
Outdoor photography 54
Portraits 62
Glamour and figure 66
Still life 70
Close-ups 75
Action shots 78
Wildlife 83
Architectural photography 86
Holiday and travel shots 90
Children and babies 94
Weddings and groups 96
Special effects 98
Night photography 102
Flowers and plants 105
Colour studies 109
Black and white photography 114
Photography at work 117
Sunsets 120
Using flash 126
The home studio 132–140
Basic lighting set-ups 135
The home darkroom 141–153
Glossary 154
Index 156

INTRODUCTION

Most people enjoy taking photographs. There are some occasions, like holidays and get-togethers with family or friends, where the camera is an indispensable part of the scene. Today's cameras, from the simplest disc or cartridge loading pocket model to the most expensive professional system, are designed to be as foolproof as possible. Yet many people are still disappointed by the results when they see the print a few days or weeks after the event.

This is because we are surrounded every day by highly professional camera images; magazines, books, television, advertisements and films. Without a little basic knowledge of how photography works, and what the camera can do, our own pictures are reduced to mere snaps. In this book you will find enough information on the how and why of photography to scale the barrier between snapshots and good photographs. The basic skills of photography, once learned, are never forgotten.

UNDERSTANDING PHOTOGRAPHY

10

THE SUBJECT

Most books on photography start by explaining how cameras and film evolved, and how they work. But this is not where photography started. It started with a very old human urge to preserve experience – to record something as fleeting as the eye's vision of the world.

Drawing began before writing, because pictures can not be passed on by word of mouth. We have no biological way to recreate images in the same way that the voice reproduces sound. To convey visual ideas verbal descriptions are needed, and these can be incomplete, inaccurate and ambiguous.

Drawing, painting and sculpture demand high levels of skill. Abstract representation is easy enough for many, but precise, accurate pictures are beyond the reach of all but the most gifted. Photography has the ability to 'catch the image in the mirror'. The principle of the *camera*, originally a room or box able to project an image of the outside world on a wall or screen, is also very old.

Over the centuries, the science of optics developed. When Canaletto painted his remarkably detailed views of Venice he did so with an artist's camera obscura – a kind of desk with a lens and a place to put sketching paper. Many portrait artists used devices like this to make sure their likenesses were close to reality.

Photography today came about as a result of experiments in the 1820s and 1830s, following a few abortive attempts earlier on, to capture permanently the image in a camera obscura. Once the basic methods had been established by Louis Daguerre (France) and W. H. Fox Talbot (Britain) photography was quick to develop. The pioneers of the 1840s became the commercial entrepreneurs of the 1850s and the artists and affluent amateurs of the 1860s and 70s. A generation after the first photograph was produced almost anyone could own and use a camera, and the turn of the century saw George Eastman's first *Kodak*, with its roll of 100 pictures. Kodak became a household name and the mystique of the photograph disappeared with the slogan 'you press the button, we do the rest'.

This brief history has a purpose – to explain, from the start, that photography is not something which exists for its own sake. It started from the quest to record and transmit what our eyes see, to share visual experiences. It started with the *subject*.

All good photographs still start with the subject. A mediocre photograph can still be of great interest if the subject is right – for example, even the most casual snap of a Victorian ancestor is now treasured. An amateur

The subject counts:
Top left: girl and coco-de-mer, by *Mike Travers*, demands repeated comparison and study.
Bottom left: a curved world from an intriguing viewpoint, by *David Kilpatrick*, uses an optical effect to interest the viewer.
Below: unfamiliar, golden-lit fish by *Monica Barnet* would be hard to describe in words where a picture succeeds.

on the spot at a newsworthy event may get a better picture than the professional pressman who arrives half an hour too late. Many important pictures have been taken by beginners on simple cameras.

This does not rule out taking an unlikely scene, and making it interesting in your photograph by using original techniques or the inherent quality of the photographic print. Some photographers have won acclaim by shooting their own shadow or rubbish in a gutter but before you can do this you have to master the art, and it is better, to begin with, to attempt to take interesting pictures.

'Good' pictures

'Oh, isn't that a good picture' is an almost meaningless comment. What is good to one person may not be to another; there are different ways of looking at pictures. A mother will like a picture of her baby because of the subject, even if it is a poor picture technically. An amusing or typical picture of any baby will probably get a warm reception from any parent but

to be praised by other photographers the picture also has to be a fine example of pose, lighting, composition, timing, and processing quality.

For some the technical quality of the picture may become the final objective. The subject is still important; a photographer who wants to show mastery of studio lighting, may find the human form is an ideal subject to display this. Another photographer who wants to show how sharp and detailed his enlarged prints are, may photograph the mechanism of an old watch instead.

Pictures like this might win awards in an exhibition but they would be unlikely to catch the eye of a sensational Sunday newspaper more interested in a blurred grab-shot of a famous personality caught off guard.

Between the two extremes of quality for its own sake, and the subject at all expense regardless of quality, there is a whole range of more balanced approaches. Take pictures of interesting subjects and aim for the best results you can manage. Be critical, and always bear in mind who is going to see the pictures.

A picture-postcard scenic view has universal appeal if the subject-matter is slightly old-fashioned or evocative of an area. This Scottish field by *David Kilpatrick* also has a strong perspective and simple composition. 35mm lens, Kodachrome 64 film.

Above: some pictures have news content which makes them interesting regardless of the technical quality. Here *Mike Travers* has captured a factory fire and attained both interest and quality.

Left: photo enthusiasts may like images with more artistic appeal than subject content. A rainy window focused through the glass by *Gordon Wigens*, who processed his own colour slide film.

THE EYE vs. THE CAMERA

The human eye has a lens, which projects an image of the outside world on to a light-sensitive retina at the back of the eyeball. The camera has a lens, which throws a similar image on to a light-sensitive film at the back of the camera. Here the resemblance of eye and camera ends. The first step to taking good pictures is to understand the differences between how the eye and camera 'sees'.

Your eyes, as a pair, see a very wide view. It is so wide that you are not conscious of an 'edge' to the picture you see. You probably think that you see everything equally clearly, but in fact only the very centre of the view – the precise point you decide to look at – is even remotely sharp. All the detail round it is very blurred. If you do not believe this, put this book on a table and look at this page from about 20cm away. Ask someone else to put their fist on the table about 60cm from the book, and to straighten out one, two, three or four fingers as they choose. Without moving your eyes, try to

count the fingers. It is impossible without cheating!

We 'see' the world round us by moving our eyes all the time. We skip, scan and jump from one detail to another, constantly. Our brains fill in the 'gaps' and make the visual image sharp and complete. The wide field of view we have, despite its very poor quality at the edges, lets us see movement and general shapes without having to look directly at them.

We can concentrate on small areas without having to move closer. A face is just as recognisable across a room as it is shaking hands with the owner. The eye can also re-focus quickly, jumping from near to far distances. It adjusts for changes in light instantly, even when deep shadows and brilliant sun are in the same scene. The eye follows rapid movement easily. All these abilities became less precise with age, and some people's eyesight is limited.

To rub home the versatility of the eye and the brain's ability to interpret

The human eye sees only a very small central part of its total field of view and you can take advantage of this. The photograph below by *Chris Mole*, has a clear focus at the centre of the image.

visual signals, rest your head sideways. The room does not suddenly tip up through 90°! Bend right over and look back through your legs, with your head upside-down. Things still look normal and you do not think the floor is now the ceiling.

The camera has qualities which are the reverse of the human eye. It takes in a small, confined view of the world; a fixed view, in a hard-edged rectangular frame. It does not scan a scene or follow movement on its own. It can not concentrate attention on one particular part of a scene. It records faithfully, with equal emphasis, all parts of the view in front of it which are correctly focused and lit.

Later on, viewing the picture, our eyes can scan across it, and concentrate on individual parts. But to start with, the camera shows no preferences. Once the shutter release is pressed, the view through the 'finder is fixed. You can not take the negative later on and include something you accidentally missed out! Nor can you eliminate

something unwanted unless it can be removed by cropping the picture.

The first thing you have to learn when handling a camera is to be aware of the frame formed by the viewfinder. It is not the centre of the viewfinder which matters, but the edges. Many people do not hold their eye close enough to the camera to see the edges, and assume that the vague rectangle formed by the eyepiece is the area they are photographing.

Every modern camera has a perfectly sharp, clear outline to show the edge of the picture through the 'finder. When composing each picture, try to fill the frame with worthwhile subject-matter. This does not mean cramming the subject in, but there is no point in a small central face surrounded by a brick wall or other unimportant background.

Some cameras have central discs, rectangles or marks like bulls' eyes in the viewfinder. These are used for focusing, to ensure that the subject is sharp and not blurred. They are not

The SLR viewfinder has a sharp, clear frame for the image and a small central focusing aid. Photograph by *Shirley Kilpatrick*, 24–35mm zoom, Ilfochrome 100 film.

'targets' for lining up the subject. You use them to set the focus, and then recompose the picture using all the viewfinder.

Colour slides may include slightly more than shown in the viewfinder. Colour prints include slightly less because some is masked off in printing. Spectacle wearers may have trouble seeing all of some viewfinders, and special correction lenses are available for most.

Finally, you have to see the view through the finder as a picture. You have to look *at*, not *through*. The image must be treated like a picture in a frame. If you hold your camera at a slight tilt (left or right hand down) the view through the finder does not tip up, so nothing looks wrong. But the viewfinder frame is tilted in relationship to the picture, and when you see the result, the tilt will show up as a sloping horizon or leaning buildings.

This is one of the most common

mistakes in photography – people leaning sideways, or the sea apparently flowing down to one edge of the shot. You *must* be aware of the frame all the time, and keep it straight. This applies whether you hold the camera normally for horizontal ('landscape format') compositions or hold it on its side for vertical ('portrait format') shots.

Before every picture, check the viewfinder frame and your composition. It will help you avoid the two most common everyday faults in pictures. These are:

a) The subject too far away, too small, dead in the centre of the picture, surrounded by irrelevant space.

b) The horizon, people, or buildings leaning like the Tower of Pisa so that shots look skewed.

These are effects that you *never* see by eye. Most people never overcome them because they have never understood why they happen.

Below left: it pays to fill the viewfinder frame with the subject, even to the extent of cropping right in and not having any significant background. Photograph by *Mick Rock*.

Below right: if a building has to be framed up from a low angle, make sure that its 'lean' is perfectly balanced so the overall effect is perpendicular. *J. J. Cornick* used a 20mm lens and a graduated tobacco-colour filter for this Ektachrome slide of Venice.

Left: a level horizon is vital when the sea is included in a shot. Picture by *Chris Mole*.

Below: some subjects do not require totally accurate camera alignment, but good composition always helps. Photograph by *E. Marsh*.

THE CAMERA

LIGHT AND FILM

Film, whether it comes in plastic cartridges, metal cassettes, flat discs or packs of instant prints, is basically the same. It may start off curled round a spool, but in every camera the film has to lie perfectly flat, behind the lens, for successful pictures to be taken.

Film is manufactured to be sensitive to light. It has to be produced, and packed, in total darkness. It stays sensitive to light until it is finally processed. It does not need batteries, chemicals or anything else to make it light-sensitive; that is built in to the film. This light-sensitivity is fixed, and unless the film is specially processed it can not be changed. Every pack of film has a figure marked on for the 'film speed'. This is written as:

ISO 125/22°

or a different figure. The important figure is the first one, in this case 125, because most cameras have a scale marked in ISO or ASA numbers. The first of the two ISO numbers is equal to the (old) ASA speed. The term ISO replaces ASA.

Film is very sensitive, because the image projected by the camera lens on to the film is fairly dim. To avoid movement of the camera or subject during the exposure, the shutter can only stay open for 1/30th of a second or shorter times. To stop action, 1/1000th of a second opening time might be needed.

Modern film cartridges and cassettes are light-proof so that you can load film in daylight, though direct sunshine should be avoided. However, accidentally opening the camera back for even a fraction of a second indoors will be enough to ruin part or all of your film.

Manufacturers constantly try to make films even more sensitive. Over the last 25 years, faster and faster films with good quality have become available. Old box cameras can not be used with ordinary modern films, and some almost-new cameras can not cope with the latest high speed films of ISO 1000/31°, because they only have settings for 100 and 400.

The ISO speed for each particular type of film is constant. Every pack you buy will be the same speed – it does not vary from production run to production run. As a general rule,

those films which are less sensitive to light or 'slow' also have the best image-quality; they have the best tones, colours, sharpness, and fineness of *grain* (the physical structure of the image).

The range of available filmspeeds is from ISO 25/15° (slow colour slide film) to ISO 1000/31° (very sensitive or 'fast' film). The two most likely speeds to be found are 100/21° or 125/22°, known as medium speed, and 400/27°, known as fast.

Film choice

There are three main types of film – *colour negative* (or print), *colour reversal* (or slide), and *black and white* negative. Colour negative film is easy to use, works in simple cameras as well as better ones, and provides colour prints at the lowest cost. Colour slides have more accurate colours, finer detail and brilliance, but have to be projected to be seen at their best. Colour prints from slides are slightly more expensive than those from negatives. Black and white film is for black and white prints only, ideal for processing and printing in your own darkroom.

Medium and *high speed* films are made in all types. Medium speed (ISO 80/20° to 200/24°) films make a good all-round choice, able to tackle most daylight conditions and give good sharpness with fine grain. High speed films (ISO 400/27° to 1600/33°) allow shooting in low light conditions without using flash, or brief shutter speeds to freeze action. *Slow* films (ISO 12/12° to 64/19°) have extra fine grain and exceptional sharpness, in black and white and colour slide form only. They are for top quality – in good light.

Above: the camera's shutter speed dial often includes a window to set the film speed. **Below:** films come in several formats including 110, disc, 35mm and 120 rollfilm sizes.

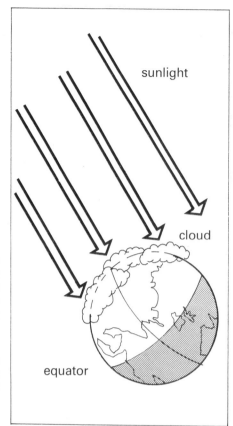

Understanding light

Without light, film can do nothing. Light, unlike film, is totally variable. It starts with the sun, which has a more or less fixed output, but as soon as the sunlight reaches us on Earth the light becomes unpredictable.

The amount of light reaching the ground depends upon the angle of the sun, clarity of the air, clouds, reflected light from ground or sea and the altitude of the location. As these factors are almost infinitely variable, we end up with a range of possible lighting conditions from full mid-day tropical sunlight on a white sandy island surrounded by sea, to a moonless night on a dark moorland landscape of Northern Europe.

Within any one scene, regardless of the lighting conditions, there will also be a range of tones and colours, unless it is totally flat and lacking in variety (like a desert landscape). Our eyes are capable of compensating for a vast range of changes in light, but unable to judge or measure actual brightness in any way.

Right: the sun is so far away from the earth that its light is always constant, but clouds and the angle of incidence create a vast range of lighting conditions from day to night.

Below: the brightest normal levels of lighting are encountered in open conditions in full sun with light surroundings and subjects. Photograph by *Hywel Phillips*.

Light meters

To make use of the film speed figure in conjunction with the camera's controls, an accurate light meter has to be used. Most cameras have one built-in. To make sure the light-meter controls the camera correctly, you must set the correct ISO speed figure first. Some cameras have a wide range (e.g. 12 to 6400) and others a choice of just two (e.g. 100 or 400). Where choice is limited either buy film to suit the camera, or set the nearest figure; for 125/22° film, set 100 if the choice is 100 or 400.

Automatic cameras make adjustments for you. Some require you to adjust one control, and the camera then sets the other. Others do everything. Some cameras are not automatic, and you adjust the controls until a needle is centred or a light goes on. The camera's settings have a fixed range, and this is why you should use a fast film when the light is poor, or for action shots. With a medium speed film there might not be enough light for the camera's available settings.

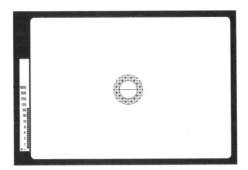

The light metering indicator through a modern SLR shows the shutter speed set by the camera's own system (**above**). A hand-held light-meter (**left**) allows selective exposure readings independent of the camera itself.

Below: the lower limits of normal meter-readings for exposure are encountered at nightfall. *Lawrence Englesberg* used a prism attachment over his wide-angle lens for this shot.

EXPOSURE AND FOCUSING

There are two camera controls used to match the fixed light-sensitivity of film to the variable brightness of light. Exposure can be adjusted in two ways: by changing the brightness of the image on the film, or by changing how long the film is exposed to the image. These two, time and brightness, are inversely proportional; halve the brightness, and you must double the exposure time. Double the brightness, and you must halve the exposure time.

This is the basis for exposure controls called the *aperture* and the *shutter*. The aperture is a circular hole behind the middle of the camera lens, which all the light reaching the film has to pass through. By using different sized holes (or having an adjustable *diaphragm* to make a continuously variable hole size) the brightness of the image passing through the lens can be altered. The shutter is simply a set of lightproof leaves which block off the light from the lens before it reaches the film. When you press the shutter release, they move aside momentarily to expose the film.

Some cameras have a lens with a fixed aperture and *shutter speed* or opening time. Exposure is only correct in good light; normally bright sunshine. Others have a fixed aperture but two or three shutter speeds; some have a fixed shutter speed, and a range of apertures. Often these simple models are marked with weather symbols to help select the settings, and have no kind of exposure metering. Cameras like this can be used in a wide range of conditions if you use different film speeds. In summer, load medium-speed film of around 100/21°.

In winter, use 400/27° film instead.

Many simple cameras use very small film sizes in 110 or disc cartridges. The fast film has much coarser grain and you can see the small dots of colour in the prints. Although using a faster film speed extends the range of lighting conditions which they can tackle, the results are inferior. This is why larger cameras, using 35mm film, are much more versatile and usually have more control over exposure.

Most *35mm cameras* have two controls. They have a lens with a variable aperture, and a shutter with a range of speeds. The exposure meter, if built-in, will be coupled to one or both.

The steps marked on the lens aperture ring and the speeds marked on the shutter dial or ring each represent a 2 × difference in light reaching the film. The film speed setting, on the other hand, is more accurate. There are three steps for every one step on the exposure controls. The film speed scale is proportional so that 200/24° is double the sensitivity of 100/21°. Some cameras just have these settings but others have intermediate settings like 100, 125, 160, 200 and so on.

When you are adjusting the controls on a camera to get the correct exposure (usually by lining up a needle or cancelling lights), never alter the film speed setting. Only move the shutter or aperture settings. These two settings have to be explained separately, and so do the various reasons why you can choose different combinations to get the same final exposure.

Below: a scene photographed with correct exposure appears as the eye sees it. A picture taken with a fixed exposure 'sunny day' camera in poor lighting comes out very grey, dark or grainy in comparison.

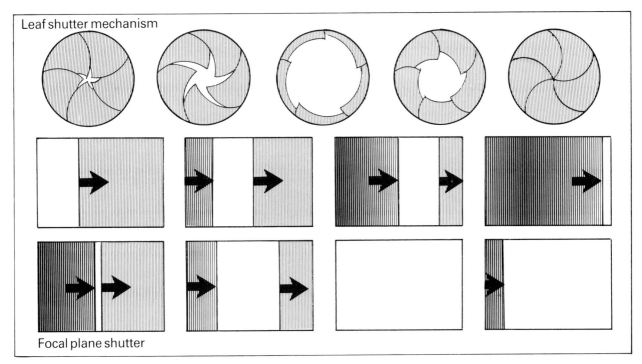

Leaf shutter mechanism

Focal plane shutter

The shutter

The shutter is extremely simple to understand. It covers the film at all times, except when an exposure is made. It is lightproof.

Because the shutter has to move aside very rapidly, and must be fairly small, the actual mechanism is highly complex. Some cameras have a shutter inside their lenses, and the best of these shutters are very intricate. They have a set of extremely thin metal blades which spring open and closed. Simple cameras may just have a metal plate with a hole in behind the lens, and a second metal plate with a hole in is pushed past at high speed.

Most 35mm *single-lens reflex* cameras, where you view through the lens instead of through a separate optical viewfinder, have a shutter immediately in front of the film, behind all the optical components and the moving viewing mirror. These shutters may be either metal or cloth, and consist of two blinds – one moves across quickly to uncover the film, and a second follows to end the exposure.

All shutters work on a time scale expressed in fractions of a second. In many cameras, with automatic shutters, you never find out what the exact exposure time is. In some, although you can not change the time yourself, the camera has a read-out in the viewfinder telling you what 'speed' has been set. In others, there is a warning sound or light when the exposure time is longer than 1/30th of a second, which is normally considered to be the longest duration which anyone can hand-hold without slight camera movement blurring the picture.

The standard time scale for shutters which you can set manually runs 1, 2, 4, 8, 15, 30, 60, 125, 250, 500, 1000. 1 stands for one second; 1000 for 1/1000th of a second. In some models, speeds are extended to longer times than 1 second – 2, 4, 8, 15, and 30. On some, they extend to shorter than 1000 to 2000 and even 4000. Many cameras do not have a full range; they may have a choice of just 1/30th and 1/125th, or a range from 1/15th to 1/250th, or perhaps an automatically-set range from 1/8th to 1/500th. You pay more for cameras with wider ranges of shutter speeds.

A full range allows photography of static subjects in dim light at times like 1 second, frozen action shots in good light at 1/1000th, and even stopping a bullet in flight at 1/4000th. The faster speeds allow high speed film to be used even in full sunlight, so one roll of film can cover all light conditions from noon to dusk.

Top: a leaf shutter mechanism consists of a set of thin metal foils which open and close very rapidly. The actual exposure is based on the time they remain fully open, after the opening process and before closing again.

Centre: a focal plane shutter, found in most SLR cameras, uses two blinds which cover the film. As one moves aside, and uncovers the film the second one follows it and covers the film again. The size of the rectangular gap created determines the exposure.

Bottom: a very narrow slit moving across the film gives 1/1000th of a second exposure (**left**). An opening half as wide as the film gives 1/125th of a second (**centre**). At 1/60th of a second, the first blind uncovers the film fully before the second one sets off. At this point, a flashgun can be fired to illuminate the whole frame.

Differential focus

If a deep zone of sharp focus is always desirable, then lenses could be left permanently stopped down in good light, and exposure controlled by the shutter alone; this is not always required. A subject can be made to stand out clearly if the background is slightly less sharp. Sometimes, the background is ugly and it helps to turn it into an abstract blur. There may also be times when pictures are taken through an unwanted foreground, like a fence at a zoo.

Differential focusing means selecting a wide aperture, like f4, to restrict sharpness to a narrow zone. Backgrounds can be blurred and obstructing wire or fences can often be lost entirely. However, any small focus error in setting the camera for the main subject will also show up more than when a closed-down aperture is used. As you can see, the aperture you set is just as important in controlling the effect in the picture as the shutter speed.

Above left: differential focus is a technique which calls for the use of a wide lens aperture to ensure that detail in front of and behind the main subject is thrown out of focus, softening the effect and concentrating attention on the important elements of the picture. Photograph of Cindy Milo by *Mike Travers*, 85mm lens, Kodachrome film. **Above right:** even in very good light, a suitable lens will give enough differential focus to avoid strongly patterned backgrounds interfering with the subject. Picture by *David Kilpatrick*, 75–150mm zoom at 135mm, Kodachrome.

Extended depth of field

The opposite of differential focus is the deliberate use of small apertures to ensure that as much of the subject as possible – or as is needed – is sharply rendered. Very wide-angle lenses have more depth of field than ordinary lenses, and these are therefore often used for special effects which call for a close-up foreground shown against an equally sharp distant scene. The sharpness can be judged on the viewing screen of any SLR camera with a depth-of-field 'stop down preview' button. With telephoto lenses, it may be impossible to ensure that every part of a deep subject is sharply rendered even at the smallest available aperture. The standard 50mm lens falls between these two extremes, so that the choice between working at f5.6 and f11 can make a great deal of difference to the final shot.

Top left: close-up detail set in a landscape context by a very wide angle lens stopped down to f16 – by *David Kilpatrick*, 17mm lens.

Lower left: a 28mm wide-angle used to original effect with minimum aperture depth by *Eric Moore*.

Above: a snowscape gets just enough depth of field to stay sharp at f8 on a 50mm lens. By *David Kilpatrick*.

Lens apertures

The aperture control on a camera is slightly harder to understand than the shutter speed control. For a start, it relates purely to relative light transmission, and not to something easily understood like a fraction of a second. To complicate matters the values which express how much light a lens lets through are written as a totally obscure series of numbers which any good mathematician will immediately understand, and other people just have to put up with.

You do not need to understand the optical theory behind the numbers engraved on your lens aperture ring. It is enough to know which way the scale runs and what each step means.

The standard scale, which is the same for every camera and every lens regardless of type, is based on this series of figures:

1, 1.4, 2, 2.8, 4, 5.6, 8, 11, 16, 22, 32, 45, 64.

These figures are called f-numbers, so you say 'f eight' or 'f one point four'. Do not confuse them with the focusing scale on your lens which is marked in feet or metres.

The only rule you need to learn is that high f-numbers mean small holes, or less light. High f-numbers have the same effect as high shutter speed numbers – they reduce exposure, for bright light. Conveniently, one aperture step equals one shutter speed step in effect. Each *stop* (as the f-number steps are called) transmits twice as much light as the next larger f-number, half as much light as the next smaller f-number. A one-stop change to the aperture has the same effect as a one-speed change to the shutter dial. Some cameras have half-way clicks between the marked f-stops to allow more accurate control.

There are one or two phrases worth knowing, referring to lens apertures:

Stop down means to use a higher f-number and reduce the amount of light reaching the film. *Open up* means the reverse. *Maximum aperture* is the widest aperture available on a particular lens. A *fast* lens has a greater maximum aperture, and can therefore be used in lower light or with faster shutter speeds. Sometimes the maximum aperture is half way between two of the normal f-numbers.

Instead of f4 or f2.8, it may be f3.5. Fast lenses are normally larger, heavier and more expensive than slower ones.

The reason why aperture steps are called f-stops is related to the *focal length* of lenses. Different focal lengths of lens produced different sized images, either to suit the size of camera or to provide *wide-angle* or *telephoto* effects. The light transmitting value of the aperture is found by dividing the diameter of hole into the focal length of the lens. If the aperture is one-eighth of the focal length, it is called f8.

The setting marked f8 on a pocket cartridge camera will be a very small hole compared with f8 on a large professional camera. The light transmission will be identical, because it is the relationship between lens focal length and aperture diameter which counts, not the actual physical size.

Right: the aperture settings on modern lenses are marked on a ring normally positioned near the camera body, and run in a sequence which is always standard.

Depth of field

The focusing scale on your camera is self-explanatory; in feet or in metres, it corresponds to the distance between the subject and the camera. If only this distance was sharply focused, pictures would be unsatisfactory. With the lens focused on a person's eyes, you would expect at the very least to have their nose and ears in focus as well.

This is what happens, of course; the lens produces a zone of sharp focus, which covers a certain amount of subject depth. The extent of this zone is called the *depth of field*, and depends on the focal length of the lens and the aperture set.

With a camera and its fixed, supplied or 'standard' lens, you only need to know that depth of field is greatest when stopped down (to f-numbers like f11 or f16) and shallowest when opened up (to

f-numbers like f4 or f2.8). Small format cameras like the disc or 110 pocket instamatic models have relatively more depth of field; large professional cameras have less. If you buy extra lenses for your camera, remember that wide angles have more depth of field and telephotos less.

Depth of field is also greater at a distance and shallower when taking close-ups. To help avoid parts of the picture going out of focus, most cameras have a simple depth of field scale. This has f-numbers engraved, to a smaller size than the aperture ring, on either side of the main index-mark for setting the focusing ring. After focusing, you read off the distances corresponding to the f-number in use, on either side of the focused distance. Anything within this zone should be sharp. Other cameras have a depth-of-field preview where the effect can be seen through the lens itself in the viewfinder.

Below: depth of field increases as the lens aperture is made smaller. The photographs show the effect of changing from a setting of f2 (top) on a 50mm lens to a setting of fl6 (bottom).

EXPOSURE METERING

Exposure controls on most cameras are coupled to a light metering system. This is a fairly simple electronic circuit which uses a light-sensitive cell which responds in the same way as film – a given brightness falling on it always produces a given effect.

At the simplest level, the exposure control is *fully automatic*. The meter is built-in and so are the controls of shutter speed, aperture or both. The user has no control over the final setting apart from adjusting the film speed to match the film in use. Even this is not always done, as cameras may have cartridges which *programme* the ISO/ASA speed automatically.

When this kind of fully automatic exposure control is fitted to an expensive camera, there may be a read-out to tell you what settings the camera has selected. Cameras like this usually have alternative ways of controlling exposure – either semi-automatic or fully manual setting of the shutter and aperture.

There are two main semi-automatic types. One is *aperture priority*; the user selects the aperture stop manually, and the camera then automatically sets the shutter speed. The other is *shutter priority*, with this logic exactly reversed.

Most camera makers call these *modes* of operation automatic although they still require a decision from the photographer. They can be found in all types of cameras, not just in 35mm single-lens reflex models; many 110 cameras use aperture priority, and 35mm compact viewfinder cameras are made with both types of automation.

Finally, there is full *manual setting*. When this uses an internal, coupled exposure meter, a needle or an array of signal lights is usually visible through the viewfinder. Scales showing the aperture and shutter scales, with pointers, may also be displayed. Without removing the camera from your eye you can adjust both controls, seeing the settings selected, to zero or centre the needle, or to change a red 'no go' light to a green 'go'.

Simpler cameras just have the needle or the lights, with no readouts or displays showing the settings. Even more basic models may have the needle in a window in the top of the camera, so that all the setting is done at waist-level.

All these methods are more convenient than hand-held, separate exposure meters. Many professionals still use these. On a separate meter, there are two scales or dials with numbers engraved on them corresponding exactly to the aperture and shutter settings on your camera. You aim the exposure meter at the subject, and a needle or light will indicate a particular reading. This reading is normally set on a scale, and then the possible choice of aperture/shutter combinations can be read off, for example – 1/125 at f8, 1/60 at f11, 1/30 at f16 and so on.

Cameras with built-in meters give less accurate readings than hand held metering, but performance is greatly improved if the light reading is taken through the camera lens itself. This is called *TTL* metering, and reads the light directly from the image which will reach the film.

Almost all 35mm single-lens reflex cameras have this feature, and hardly any other types include it. Larger format professional cameras may have an option to add it.

Opposite: *Martin Lillicrap* set up a bare filament light bulb in a darkened room and added flash to light the edges of the glass envelope and the holder, with a diffraction grating on the camera lens to produce the rainbow patterns, expressing the essence of light, colour and exposure.

Below: the optical path of a typical 35mm camera allows light to be diverted for a meter reading at various different points – on the mirror surface itself (A); off the film (B); via a secondary mirror (C); through a beamsplitter in the focusing screen (D); in the top of the prism optics (E) or close to the viewing eyepiece (F).

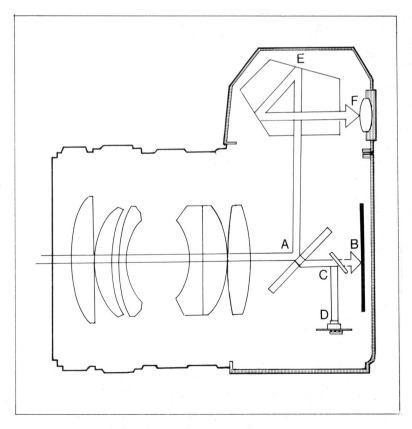

Using exposure meters

The idea of the exposure meter is to judge the amount of light reaching the film. As the average picture is a scene with about one-third of the area blue sky, some face tones, and the rest grass or ground, meters are calibrated to give the best results from this average type of subject.

Things go wrong when instead of a neutral, ordinary scene you decide to photograph something different. The most frequent error creeps in when instead of a blue sky and a sunny scene, you have a dull day with a plain white sky. This is much brighter in relation to the ground than a blue sky on a sunny day. The meter assumes the bright sky is a rather well-lit subject. It recommends the ideal exposure to show all the detail – in the sky. This is why and how you end up with black faces, grey ground, and glowering grey skies.

The reverse happens when you shoot a person standing in a large, dark open doorway. The meter is influenced by the expanse of empty black, recommends extra exposure, and the person ends up bleached white. These are the main situations where an exposure meter, or metering system, will give incorrect results:

A very light overall subject
A very dark overall subject
A bright background
A dark background
Too much sky included
No sky whatsoever included
Spotlighting (on stage)
Backlighting – sun behind the subject
Light sources included in the picture or metered area

The best way to overcome these problems is to take a selective meter reading from an average-toned area. If there is a hazy, bright sky, aim downward and read from the ground. If the subject is against a very dark or light background, move closer and read from the subject only. If the subject is very light or dark, take a reading from your own hand in the same light and position.

Below: a very light overall subject with high contrast would normally end up recording as dull grey. By taking a meter reading from the riverbank rather than the very difficult telephoto view of a semi-silhouetted subject on water, correct exposure was ensured for this picture. By *David Kilpatrick*, 100–300mm zoom, FP4 film.

Your skin is probably about the right tone for an average reading, but do not go to the extent of refocusing the lens on your hand if you are using an SLR; just meter from the blurred image. These methods work well with manual control, or hand-held meters. If your camera is automatic, some means of taking a selective reading and locking it is needed.

Some cameras have a *hold* or *memory* button, so that you can move close or aim the camera down, press the button to take a reading, hold it, move back to compose the shot you want, and fire. Others will lock the reading if you half-press the shutter, keeping your finger on it while re-composing and finally firing.

Once you get to know how a camera or exposure meter behaves when confronted with difficult light, you can adjust the metered exposure instead of taking a selective reading. This is a good solution when every shot you take is in untypical lighting – for example, when photographing aircraft at an air show against a cloudy sky.

The simplest form of adjustment is a *backlight* button. You press this whenever the background is too bright or the light shines towards the camera, and it increases the exposure by $1\frac{1}{2}$ to $2\times$ (depending on make). Other cameras have an *over-ride* dial with a central 'normal' setting, and marks on either side for $+1$ and $+2$, -1 and -2. Moving the dial to $+1$ increases the exposure by one stop (equal to one aperture or shutter interval, or $2\times$); $+2$ is two stops $(4\times)$. Similarly, -1 reduces the amount of light reaching the film by one stop $(1/2)$, and -2 by two stops $(1/4)$. These are the *factors* by which the exposure is changed. If you set the dial to $+1$ and leave it, then every single picture you take until it is returned to zero will receive twice the normal exposure.

In the case of aeroplanes against the sky you would set the dial to $+1$ and leave it until you started to take pictures of normal average scenes again. At a zoo, with animals photographed against dark cage backgrounds and no sky in the pictures, an over-ride setting of -1 is suitable. Always remember to cancel over-ride after using it! Not all cameras have a warning light in the viewfinder!

Remembering exactly when to use the exposure adjustment controls, or take a selective exposure reading, can be hard. The rule of thumb is that when there seems to be too much light in the background, when the sun is in your eyes or the subject is against bright snow or sand, give PLUS; extra exposure. When the background is dark and the subject seems too dull for the meter to give a decent reading, give MINUS; less exposure.

The exception to this rule is when you actually want the result to be wrong. If you want to show extra detail in a naturally dark subject, just

Above: an average meter reading from this scene would be too influenced by the dark doorway it is taken from, resulting in a bleached-out sunlit area. A close-up reading from a sunny spot would go the other way, and make the doorway too dark. *Dave Crisp* used a meter reading from the shadow area on the street, and obtained a perfect balance.

give the exposure recommended by your meter. The same applies if you want a black silhouette against the sky, instead of detail in the subject.

If you use colour negative film for prints, small errors in exposure have little effect on the final result. The same applies to black and white. Exposure adjustment is very important, however, with colour slide film, as the final slide depends entirely on your original exposure.

Selecting settings

Even if your camera is semi-automatic, using shutter or aperture priority, you have a choice to make. The camera will give an equally 'correct' exposure with the shutter speed at 1/1000 and the aperture at f2.8, or the shutter speed at 1/30 and the aperture at f16. These combinations are identical in the amount of light they allow to reach the film.

They are very different in terms of the final results, though, and you have to be able to make some simple

decisions about shutter speed and aperture before you can guarantee good results.

Take the first combination: 1/1000 at f2.8. The shutter speed is totally 'safe'; you can hand-hold 1/1000 and be sure of sharp pictures even if you are shooting from a moving vehicle. But aperture is a problem. Apart from controlling the light transmission, different aperture settings change the depth of field. At wide apertures like f2 or f2.8 distance setting must be very accurate, and only a limited zone will be sharp.

In single-lens reflex cameras you view and focus through the lens at its maximum aperture. The shallow depth of field means that the subject snaps sharply into focus as you hit the correct setting. Everything else is blurred. When the picture is taken, the aperture diaphragm in the lens closes down rapidly to the *working aperture* pre-set on the aperture scale. If you want to judge the true depth of field, after focusing, some models have a

Below: an aperture-priority auto camera is ideal for shots where the depth of field is important, and a small f-stop like f16 can be selected. Kodachrome slide by *Don Ralston*.

depth of field *stop-down preview* which closes the aperture down, allowing you to see the effect through the viewfinder.

Because of the differential focus effect, the view through an SLR finder may hide problems unless you use the preview or look critically at the scene by eye. A telegraph pole in the distance may not be apparent through the finder, because it is so blurred, but could appear to grow out of someone's head in the final print. Choosing the aperture depends to an extent on the acceptable shutter speed. With a static subject and a tripod, you can use any shutter speed you like. With a hand-held camera, any speed longer than 1/30th is likely to mean unsharp pictures through camera shake.

Most pictures in good daylight can be taken at shutter speeds around 1/125th and apertures in the middle of the scale, around f8. There is little risk of camera shake and the depth of field is adequate for everything but the closest subjects. There is still some

differential focus to help make the subject stand out.

If the picture includes movement, then either 1/250 at f5.6 (running, distant cars, boats, cyclists moving slowly) or 1/500 at f4 (normal traffic, athletes, aircraft, children running and jumping near the camera) can be used. If depth of field is very important – perhaps to include a bed of flowers and a house in the background both in sharp focus – then 1/30th at f16 would be better.

In general the extreme ends of the shutter and aperture scales are only needed to cope with extreme conditions – very bright light, fast action, very dim light, exceptional subject depth, or a need to throw a background totally out of focus. Most pictures can be taken using a range of settings limited to 1/60, 1/125, 1/250, f5.6, f8 and f11.

Below: *Ian Buckden* selected a fast shutter speed and a relatively wide lens aperture for this shot of vintage motorcycle combination racing, taken on high-speed Ektachrome film with a telephoto zoom lens.

EQUIPMENT

CHOOSING A CAMERA

Different types of camera have been mentioned already because they have different technical features or controls. The biggest differences in terms of final result are made by the size and type of film used.

Instant cameras are large, and take packs of eight or ten sheets of a special material which provides a print about a minute after the shot is taken. No other cameras do this. Extra copies must either be taken at the time separately, or duplicated from the print. There is no negative to keep.

Pocket cameras use very compact cartridges containing a film or disc. The negatives are small, and only suitable for making prints about 8 × 10cm. Although some precision cameras of this type exist they are not intended for enthusiasts, and home processing and printing is not advisable.

Subminiature cameras are even smaller, but normally made to high precision and specification. Special processing and printing equipment is made for home use, and it is considered a worthwhile technical challenge to tackle this.

35mm cameras use perforated film in lightproof cassettes, normally with a negative size of 24 × 36mm. This is the smallest format suitable for professional photography, and the best choice for good quality amateur pictures. The range of different 35mm camera types is enormous.

120 rollfilm cameras are larger, and used mainly by advanced amateurs and professionals. The equipment is expensive, but there are many good secondhand folding rollfilm cameras available to allow experiment with the larger film size

Both 35mm and 120 rollfilm are ideal for home processing and printing. The smaller 35mm size is easier to handle and the equipment costs less.

Large format cameras range from film size 6 × 9.5cm to 20 × 24cm, but the most popular size is 9 × 12cm (5 × 4″). They are used by professionals when quality, regardless of cost or convenience, is demanded. There are other types of camera, and various other film sizes, which you are unlikely to come across or use.

Basic types

There are two main types of camera: viewfinder models, fitted with a separate optical system to view through, and reflex cameras where the viewfinder uses the same lens system that forms the image on the film.

If you have poor eyesight, a viewfinder camera may prove easier to use. Some have simple scale or symbol focusing, by guessing or judging the distance. Others have a focusing aid in the viewfinder producing a double image when out of focus, merging into a single image after correct focusing. Auto-focusing does away with the need for any judgment and is ideal for people with eyesight problems.

Reflex cameras allow much more accurate composition and focusing, and have interchangeable lenses. Exposure, focus, depth of field and precise composition regardless of distance can be checked through the finder before taking the shot. Some reflex cameras offer a choice of viewing at eye-level, through an eyepiece, or at waist level by looking down on to a focusing screen. This can be useful for changing viewpoints.

Popular reflex cameras have focusing screens with central focusing aids, exaggerating the changes in the image when it goes out of focus. *Split-image* rangefinders move adjacent details out of line, and only line them up when focused. *Microprism* rangefinders make the image appear to shimmer when out of focus. The shimmering disappears when correctly focused.

One disadvantage of the SLR (single lens reflex) design is that a mirror which diverts the lens image into the viewfinder has to swing away before exposure. The moving mirror makes more noise and vibration than viewfinder cameras. Modern designs damp this down very effectively.

Some 120 rollfilm reflexes use two lenses, in parallel, to avoid this. They are called TLRs or twin-lens reflexes. Reflexes are available in simple point-and-shoot form as well as high specification, fully manual types with large systems of accessories and lenses. Automatic focusing is optional on some.

Opposite page: cameras come in many shapes and sizes. Top shelf – popular types include pocket, disc and instant-picture cameras. Middle shelf – the mainstream 35mm field includes fully automatic single-lens reflexes with oufits of lenses alongside simple compact and pocketable models. Bottom shelf: rollfilm cameras are intended for the highest quality compatible with acceptable cost and portability, and match 35mm SLRs in their range of accessories and lenses.

'One-touch' cameras

The most popular and easily-used 35mm cameras are 'one-touch' models. Though the term used to describe them is new, the idea isn't; ever since the early 1960s there have been 35mm models with programmed exposure and automatic shutters, motor film wind and coupled focusing.

The current cameras are much smaller and far better, and they have automatic film loading and unloading as well as motor wind. The focusing is fully automatic – point and shoot – instead of coupled to the viewfinder or using symbols. The exposure system is not much different but many cameras set the film speed by sensing a code on any 'DX' type 35mm cassette. These cassettes are an international standard type which links to electrical contact pins inside the camera to tell it the type of film, film speed, number of exposures on the roll, and how much error is allowable in exposure.

Most one-touch cameras also have a built-in flash which may come into action as soon as the light gets too low for hand held shooting. The advantage of a one-touch 35mm model is that even with gloves on and only one hand free, you can raise a camera to your eye and shoot. The camera will set the focus, set the exposure, turn on the flash if necessary, take the picture and wind on to the next frame.

Most cameras like this have a slightly wide angle lens, suitable for general scenes and shots of small groups in domestic settings. They do not have interchangeable lenses but you may be able to get simple 'tele' and 'wide' or 'close-up' kits for them. Usually the closest focusing distance is about 75cm (2'6") and this is just about right for a shot of a baby or a rather close portrait.

One-touch cameras are so useful because they can catch expressions and action easily, and the results are often equal to those from 35mm single lens reflexes when used under similar conditions.

Below: the compact one-touch 35mm camera is ideal for catching natural shots of people using a fast film. Photograph by *Raymond Lea*.

Left: examples of 35mm one-touch cameras include models which have a built-in 'case' opening for operation, others which are less complex and mechanically simpler, and the most basic models which do not need focusing for the simple reason that the focus itself is fixed on a single, set average distance.

Below left: the 35mm lens fitted to most one-touch cameras is wide enough for general shots at work, but you may not be able to get all the subject in.

Below right: the closest focusing distance of slightly under one metre is ideal for outdoor portraits. Both photographs by *David Kilpatrick.*

Automatic SLRs

The auto SLR is the main form of 35mm camera for the serious photographer as well as the best choice for most everyday photography. The latest models have as many automated features as one-touch cameras and can actually be used as if they were simple cameras.

Straightforward auto-exposure SLRs may be shutter-priority or aperture-priority. The 'priority' part means that the user has control over this particular one of the two exposure controls, and the camera then sets the other. A shutter priority camera is ideal for action and sports work – you can set 1/500th of a second as a shutter speed, and the camera then changes the aperture of the lens to cope with changing light. An aperture priority camera is better for landscapes, close-ups and portraits because you can set an aperture to give the correct control of sharpness in depth, and the camera then varies the shutter speed.

Programmed exposure setting is a combination, very much as on one-touch cameras, which sets both controls for you on a fixed scale. You may have a choice of programmes for action, wide-angle views and so on or the camera may change the programme according to the lens.

Focus-check is a feature which tells you, by means of a set of 'traffic lights' in the viewfinder, when you have set the focusing exactly. Auto focusing is a stage further which sets the lens using a small motor, so that there is no need to do anything except line up the subject. For people with good eyesight, these aids may not be necessary, but for anyone whose vision is less than perfect they are very useful. Auto focus is also invaluable for some types of action and candid photography where the camera must be targeted on the subject very quickly, with little time to adjust anything manually.

The DX cassette sensing feature of one-touch 35mms is now available on several single-lens reflexes as well, often in an extended form which will cope with a vast range of possible films.

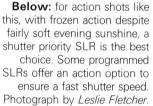

Below: for action shots like this, with frozen action despite fairly soft evening sunshine, a shutter priority SLR is the best choice. Some programmed SLRs offer an action option to ensure a fast shutter speed. Photograph by *Leslie Fletcher.*

The final parts of current automatic SLRs are the motordrive and command functions, and flash. In some models the motor drive to wind the film is built-in, but in others you have a choice of compact medium-speed (1.5 to 2.5 frames each second) winders and full motor drives (3 to 5 frames per second) which may even use a separate battery pack.

Command systems link to the motor drive and the exposure and shutter release controls. Most of these take the form of replacement camera backs, which can imprint data on the film but also programme in a sequence of timed shots. A command data back of this type can ask the camera to take ten shots in a row at ten second intervals, starting at 9.30pm, and to switch the flash system on if necessary!

Flash in most new SLRs is 'dedicated', which means that as long as the electronic flashgun is matched correctly to the SLR body, it will set the shutter to the correct speed, read off what film is loaded, and give fully automatic correct exposure which in many cases is metered from the film surface during the exposure itself.

Dedicated flashguns like this sometimes just attach to the camera's 'hot shoe' on and form an extension of the camera body, but more often they can be removed from the camera using special cables and two or three flashguns can be arranged to produce attractive lighting, all linked with connector boxes. Special flashguns can be used to light extremely close subjects and professional guns with large battery packs allow you to shoot many hundreds of pictures rapidly.

The advantages of owning an SLR, especially a fairly recent model with a good range of exposure 'modes' and features like the motor drive and dedicated flash, are considerable.

With an SLR, any image which can be formed on the film can also be viewed through the viewfinder – even when using a microscope, telescope, or an underwater casing for the camera. This opens up a vast range of possibilities, and by far the most important ones are covered by the many ranges of interchangeable lenses made for SLRs.

Below: with a 35mm SLR, you can photograph almost anything you can see, including images through microscopes and telescopes. Nothing more than a normal close-up lens is required for shots like this peacock feather by *Gordon Wigens*.

When you look through a camera with a separate viewfinder, the effect of the lens is not obvious. Most optical finders provide a neat, slightly reduced image, but this does not bear an exact relationship to the lens's view, which is from a slightly different position.

When the subject is a distant view, this has no effect. Close up, the difference of a few centimetres can be enough to mean that the viewfinder image needs correcting. Marks are engraved, showing the limits of accuracy at the closest focus, to help avoid cut-off heads or off-centre subjects.

Most cameras with separate viewfinders have a fixed lens, which can not be changed. Some 110 models have a pair of lenses, normal and portrait or telephoto, which slide into place. The fixed lens on a 35mm viewfinder camera is generally one taking in about 60° diagonally, a wide enough angle for shots of small groups of people in normal rooms. Most flashguns will cover this angle acceptably, but would not manage a wider field of view.

This angle of view is very natural. It corresponds to the angle of view you see when standing back and looking at a distant scene. However, it is wider than the angle you concentrate on when talking to someone face to face; it tends to include rather too much surrounding detail. The focal length of lens giving this effect, on 35mm film, is around 38mm. The standard lens fitted when you buy a 35mm SLR is a *50mm*. This is slightly more selective, and allows better close-ups, but can be restricting when photographing groups of people, buildings or other subjects needing a wider view. The coverage of a 50mm lens is 43° diagonally.

Lenses with a *shorter* focal length than 50mm on 35mm film are all called wide-angles, and take in more of the view, showing everything smaller. Lenses *longer* than 50mm are termed *long focus* and show less, to a larger scale. Any lens with a variable image size, whether wide or tele, is termed a zoom. Some people think 'zoom' lenses have to be long focus. *Telephoto* lenses are long focus lenses made to a more compact design, so that the lens is physically shorter than its focal length.

Below: different lenses for 35mm SLRs give different fields of view ranging from a wide-angle scene to a strong close-up. Using this picture by *David Mark*, the relative coverage of lenses from 24mm to 135mm is shown.

Medium telephotos

It's hard to categorize ranges of focal lengths easily, but the medium telephoto is normally the sort of lens you can carry in a corner of a camera bag and hold by hand, which does not need a tripod for good results. This means any lens with a focal length from 75mm to 200mm, or about 1.5× to 4× magnification compared to the standard 50mm lens.

The shortest length normally found is the *85mm* or *90mm*, as there is not enough difference between a 50mm and 75mm to make it worth owning such a close match. There are two types of 85/90mm lens – ones intended for portraiture which are also very wide in maximum aperture and ideal for news photography, and ones for close-up work.

The typical 85mm portrait lens is f1 or f1.4, a little larger than the standard 50mm, and gives a very easy-to-focus bright image through the viewfinder. Many people find the extra magnification and the excellent quality of such lenses makes them an alternative to the 50mm, for use on most subjects.

The macro 90mm (as most are) usually focuses down to half life size or even life size without accessories. The typical maximum aperture is f3.5 to f2.5, and once again the quality is often superb, but the lens may be large and heavy. The benefit of a special close-focusing lens which is also a telephoto is that you can take a close-up of an insect or flower from slightly further away than normal, avoiding disturbing the subject or casting your own shadow over it. These lenses are perfectly suitable for general use as well.

The 'short tele' 100 or 105mm is usually a fast lens – f2.8 to f2 – and extremely light and compact, while giving a 2× magnification compared to the 50mm. Most lenses like this focus down to around 1 metre, and can be used for shots of pets, children, portraits, sports, landscapes and all kinds of subjects. They are pocketable and give very good quality, but like the 85/90mm they don't have a dramatic effect through the viewfinder and are less popular than more powerful telephotos.

Above: a 100mm telephoto was used for this outdoor still life shot in the village of Les Baux, in Provence, by *David Kilpatrick.*

Left: lenses around 85–100mm are ideal for scenic views like this lakeside scene by *J. L. Smith.*

The 'standard' telephoto is the 135mm, for many decades considered the ideal all-purpose lens for hand held tele shooting. They are not very compact but are often fairly light and easy to handle, with aperture of f2.8 or f3.5 in most cases but some available as f2 or faster – and very heavy to go with the extra light-gathering power. The main difference between the 100mm and the 135mm is often in the contrast and colour saturation of the

picture, and the closest focusing. Most 135mms stop short at around 1.5 metres. Though at this distance they give a really full-face portrait or pick out a small subject, it can be difficult when a moving target suddenly comes closer than the 1.5 metre limit. 135mms are perfect for travel, action sports, candids and as a lightweight lens when you only want to have one telephoto with you.

The *200mm*, considered the longest

Right: a zoom lens was set to 135mm to catch an atmospheric shot of horses grazing in the Camargue, with differential focus at f4, and a diffusing filter. By *David Kilpatrick*.

focal length you can hold by hand with reasonable results, blows up just one-eighth of the normal 50mm view (a 4× linear magnification) and the image through the viewfinder is therefore fairly impressive.

With a good 200mm lens, you can tackle domestic wildlife photographs like birds feeding on a table 2–3 metres away, and take pictures at events where the subject is at a controlled distance, like air shows and motor sports. The 200mm is also ideal for use in zoos, on safari trips, and where your subject may be hostile and it's best to go unnoticed. The average 200mm is around f3.5 in maximum aperture and focuses to 2.5 metres, but some will focus much closer and fast f2.8 versions are available for floodlit sports or theatre and concert photography. The 200mm is about the shortest telephoto which will give you a shot of a sunset with the sun looking 'big' as you think you see it with the naked eye.

Left: a classic use of the 200mm lens is outdoor 'street' candid photography. This picture is titled 'Black and White'.

Below: air show shots – this one has been combined with a sunset slide – need lenses of around 200mm. Both pictures by *Lawrence Englesberg*.

Opposite: A 17mm wide-angle lens used very close to this tribesman helped create a dramatic action image for photographer *Bruce Davidson*, working on location with the Masai in Kenya and covering tribal dances and rituals.

Below left: a 50–135mm telephoto zoom lens was used at its full 135mm focal length to set the towers of the Alhambra against a floral foreground. Photograph by *Shirley Kilpatrick.*

Below right: many zoom lenses have a macro facility which enables excellent close-ups, especially when stopped down to a small aperture and using flash. Photograph by *Ken Meanwell.*

Long focus zooms

Tele-zooms normally cover precisely the range from 75–200mm and are therefore the entire set of medium tele lenses rolled into one. A typical 70–210mm zoom (just exceeding the range) will have an f3.5 maximum aperture and be about 25% larger and heavier than a similar 200mm lens.

Zooms have advantages. Apart from carrying a single lens in place of four, they fill in all the gaps between the 85/100/135/200 fixed focal lengths. Much long-focus photography is done at a fixed distance, standing in a spot where you are not able to move freely, or in crowds. The zoom enables you to frame up and adjust the composition exactly without having to move your viewpoint.

Most zooms also focus closer than most 200mm lenses, often down to less than 1 metre. This is necessary for the shorter focal lengths like 70mm or 100mm to be fully usable. The bonus is that the focusing also applies at the 'long' end, and a good 70–210mm zoom will focus close enough to copy a postcard. Some have an additional 'macro' setting which moves a group of lens elements so that the lens can focus on very small subjects like butterflies or flowers. The disadvantages of the zoom over this range are mainly to do with size; if you intend to carry a 200mm, then a 70–210mm is hardly any different, but if you plan to pocket a lightweight 85/100mm the zoom is three or four times as big.

Such large and imposing lenses are not ideal for portraiture, and may get in the way when working quickly. The maximum aperture can also be limited when compared with a fast 85mm, and focusing in dim light with zooms may be much harder. Finally, the optical quality of zoom telephotos is excellent but always a step behind that of separate 'prime' telephotos; any improvements which can be made to a new generation of zooms will allow separate lenses to be improved as much.

Wide-angles

Some attempt is made to classify wide-angles into wide, super wide and ultra wide. As the total range of available wide-angles is from 14mm to 35mm, this is a fairly exact categorization. Lenses of 35mm and 28mm focal length are just called 'wide'. Lenses from around 20mm to 25mm are called 'super wide', and those from 14mm to 19mm 'ultra wide'. The practical limits of ordinary lenses found for most SLRs are between 17mm and 35mm, though in some makes nothing longer than a 28mm is available.

With teles, you can think of magnifications like 2× or 4×. With wides, it is not as easy. A 25mm lens does take in an angle of view twice that of the 50mm standard, but the effect through the viewfinder is much more dramatic than you might imagine. Most people find that a 35mm lens, giving the same field of view as most one-touch cameras, is not sufficiently different from a standard 50mm. There are good reasons for owning a 35mm instead of a 50mm if you photograph many groups of people.

The *28mm* is the ideal wide-angle for general use, often with a maximum aperture between f2 and f2.8, and with no over-dramatic stretching of the subject towards the edges of the picture. By careful handling a 28mm can produce shots which look very wide-angle in effect, or perfectly ordinary.

The *24mm* may not seem very different but in practice, it produces the 'wide-angle feel' most of the time and it is a major effort to produce shots without this effect. It is not suitable for groups or for flash pictures.

Some flashguns have adaptors to enable them to cover the field of the 24mm lens, but unless you are shooting a fairly distant group or a room interior, using flash with such a wide-angle lens may give unpleasantly empty background shadows. This is because your flash is so close to the main subject.

The *20/21mm* begins to be a specialist lens, ideal for architecture and some types of dramatic scenic and

travel pictures. A 20mm shot is often characterized by a feeling of distance, deep blue skies, and of scale. This is a lens which estate agents use to show off houses and gardens to their best advantage. As with the 24mm, the typical maximum aperture will be around f2.8 and the size of the lens is often about the same as a 50mm.

Choose a *17, 18 or 19mm* and the size of the optical groupings goes up – with a drop in aperture. A typical 17mm will be around f4 with twice the size of front glass element of a 20mm. The viewfinder image may be fairly dark and focusing is usually difficult with these lenses.

Long telephotos

Almost anyone can handle extreme wide-angle lenses successfully from the technical point of view; they produce sharp pictures even when focusing and camera steadiness leave something to be desired.

Very long focus lenses, from 250mm to 1000mm and even more, often disappoint inexperienced users because they are hard to use properly. A fast shutter speed is essential, to prevent camera shake blurring the image. Focusing is so selective that only a few inches of depth may be sharp at a distance of many yards. Because the very long telephoto picks out a small

Right: the mirror telephoto lens, or catadioptric lens, is a very compact form which creates a distinctive kind of image. Here, out of focus points of light are rendered as floating 'doughnuts'. Photograph by *David Kilpatrick*, 500mm f8 RF Rokkor lens.

part of a scene, the exposure in that particular part may be different from the general lighting condition elsewhere. Mist, haze or even rising warm air on a hot day can degrade the image; shooting through ordinary window glass is enough to make focusing impossible in some cases.

Long telephotos are also large, heavy and limited in maximum aperture. A typical lens suitable for photographing small wildlife or distant sports is a 400mm; normally they are no 'faster' than f5.6, and the focusing aids in a typical SLR viewing screen go black and can not be used normally. You can buy lenses like a 300mm f2.8 or 500mm f4 but these may cost ten to twenty times the price of ordinary versions.

There are a few solutions for everyday users who want to try these specialist lenses. The first is the *mirror lens*, a specially compact version of a long telephoto normally between 250mm and 1000mm, with a maximum aperture between f5.6 and f11. As mirror lenses cost relatively little and weigh even less, they are easily handled with a light tripod. They are best used with an automatic SLR on aperture priority. A second is the *tele converter*, which also costs little

in comparative terms and fits behind a normal medium telephoto or zoom and doubles its focal length(s).

A 1.4× teleconverter turns a 200mm f4 lens into a 280mm, but at the same time reduces its maximum f-stop to f5.6. A 2× converter turns the same lens into a much more impressive 400mm, but cuts the aperture to f8. Converters are made to match many zooms, and give the best quality with one lens in particular. Others are made for general use and are a compromise, fitting all lenses with the same mount but giving a slight quality loss.

The best solution to the problems encountered with these long telephotos and 'extended' zooms is to use a very fast film speed like ISO 1000. This makes sure your shutter speed is as high as possible. The Minolta 7000 camera actually reads off the focal length of the lens in use, and with long telephotos, automatically switches to a fast shutter speed. More cameras are likely to have this kind of coupling in future so that results from long lenses become more consistent for beginners and less experienced users. Some general guidelines can, in the meantime, be useful for using different focal lengths.

Left: some subjects are simply not accessible from close distances, and a lens of 200–500mm is essential to ensure strong close-ups. In this shot *Duncan McEwan* has used a very high shutter speed to freeze action totally.

Lenses in use

Life would be very simple if every lens, whether wide-angle or telephoto, behaved in exactly the same way. Both types have characteristics, and handling problems which need understanding. It is easier to use popular 'moderate' focal lengths at first, because the effects and problems are not extreme.

Wide-angles have great depth of field and this makes critical focusing harder, because the image does not seem to snap in and out of focus as clearly. On the other hand, small errors in setting have less effect. Differential focus often can not be obtained, so intrusive backgrounds can not be thrown into unsharpness.

Because wide-angle lens shots often include more sky, through-the-lens meter readings may be influenced. It is important to use selective readings, memory hold or over-ride with wide-angles. Tilting a wide-angle lens up or down to photograph a building or perhaps a child produces strongly converging or diverging verticals, a 'leaning backwards' or 'big head' effect.

To avoid this, keep the camera aiming straight ahead as if it was fitted with a spirit level. For example, to photograph a young child, drop down to kneeling position. To photograph a building, get far enough back to avoid having to tilt the camera upwards, or find an elevated viewpoint.

Long-focus lenses seem very easy to focus through the SLR finder. There is a point of critical sharpness and even a small change in focus setting, subject position or camera position loses this. They have very shallow depth of field. Small focusing errors can spoil a picture, and it is worth trying to use closed-down apertures to increase the depth of field.

Because the detail of the subject is magnified compared to the standard lens, any subject movement or camera shake will show up to a greater extent. The only way to reduce the risk is to use a faster shutter speed than normal. As a guide, never use a speed lower (numerically) than the focal length of the lens in millimetres. With a 50mm lens, 1/60th is a fast enough speed too avoid camera shake and freeze normal movements like changes of facial expression.

With a 100mm lens, 1/125th is the slowest speed you should use; with a 135mm or 200mm, 1/250th, and so on.

Left: *Mike Baker* was able to secure a sharp image in poor lighting conditions, by ensuring his shutter speed with a 50mm lens was 1/125.

As your are also trying to use closed-down f-stops to increase the limited depth of field, a fast film (ISO/ASA 400/27°) is very useful for long focus work. Medium speed films can be used with confidence on bright, sunny days. If you want to use slow films with long lenses, a tripod is almost essential. Lenses over 200mm are normally fitted with a tripod thread because most shots taken with them will need some kind of firm support.

Many long focus shots end up over-exposed, although it is best to give the minimum acceptable exposure in order to ensure the fastest shutter speed possible. This is because telephoto lens views often include no sky, and the meter indicates too much exposure.

It can help to set camera over-ride controls to give half the normal exposure (-1) when using telephoto lenses for shots which include no sky. The only exception is when the background or a frame-filling subject are evenly light in tone – like sea, sand, or a full frame shot of a face.

Sets of lenses

Exact focal lengths matter when choosing an outfit of lenses. The only way to grasp what they mean in practice is to visit a dealer, and look through a camera fitted in turn with a range of lenses. The most useful lenses to start with, if you already own a 50mm standard, are the 28mm wide-angle and 135mm telephoto. There are some excellent 24–35mm zooms, and some equally good 70–150mm zooms, which give versatility around these basic focal lengths.

Most people would then add a 200mm telephoto to an outfit, or pick a 70–200mm zoom instead. Bear in mind that most good 70–200mm zooms are far bigger than a simple 135mm but most 70–150mm zooms are the same size.

A 20mm wide-angle gives a very dramatic view. You should be content with a 24mm as your widest angle of lens unless you are after unusual pictures or intend to specialize in architectural shots. Telephotos longer than 200mm take some handling, but there are several excellent lightweight 'mirror' lenses available in lengths from 250 to 600mm.

Anything longer than 600mm or shorter than 20mm can be classed as a special lens. You would probably find a 1000mm tele impossible to use, but you might enjoy the strange effects from a 17mm wide-angle (105° of view) or a 16mm fish-eye (180°, and the world resembles a curved barrel).

It is not necessary to own every lens in a range to take good photographs. If you have a camera fitted with a standard 50mm lens, a 28mm wide angle and 135mm telephoto will complete a compact and versatile outfit. A 200mm telephoto and 20mm wide angle would give you a very wide range of effects and approaches indeed.

Some people would prefer a single long focus zoom like an 80–200mm in place of two telephotos, perhaps adding a longer mirror lens. Others like wide-angle shots, and could find a 24–35mm zoom ideal. If you are interested in flower and insect close-ups, there are special lenses which focus very close. Some zooms have this feature built-in. Special 'macro' close-up lenses are made (at a price) for the best possible detail sharpness.

Care of lenses

Nearly all modern SLR lenses produce sharp, brilliant results with accurate colour. They are precision assemblies, even if mass-produced, and should be treated with care.

Protect your lenses with cases if supplied, and use the lens caps. A 'clear' haze or skylight filter fitted to the front will prevent damage by dust, spray or accidental knocks. If you allow the front glass surface of the lens to become dirty, dusty, wet or scratched your pictures will lose contrast and look dull, misty and flat.

Lenses should be cleaned using proper lens tissue after first blowing away any dust and grit with a blower-brush. Never rub a lens hard; never use a piece of tissue twice; and never use household tissues! Have the caps ready to cover exposed rear mounts when changing lenses. Do not place a lens on a table so that it can roll off. Do not change lenses on a cold camera in a humid atmosphere, especially if the lens has misted up; condensation could form inside the camera and even on the film itself.

In addition to lenses, carrying cases and a tripod you will probably need a flashgun, some filters and other minor accessories.

Flashguns range in size from slim units you can slip in a pocket to big 'hammer-head' guns with separate power packs slung over your shoulder. The size is directly related to power output.

For normal photography, you should try to acquire a flashgun with a power rated as *GN30 metric*. This will handle almost all occasions. The GN (guide number) is a figure which expresses the power output from a flashgun, which in turn decides the kind of lens apertures you have to use and the maximum distance you can stand from the subject.

If the GN is quoted in feet, look for figures around 80 to 100 at ISO 100/21°. This is around the same as the 28 to 30 needed if the figure is quoted for metres. This gives you enough power in reserve to ensure well exposed shots, even of fairly large groups or outdoors where much of the light from the flash is lost.

Flashguns mount on to the camera using a shoe. Larger models have brackets to avoid strain on the camera and improve handling and balance. Some cameras do not have separate flash cable sockets for these, and an adaptor must be fitted into the camera's 'hot shoe' which has the only flash connnection. Most SLRs have both.

Dedicated flash units have extra connections which couple to the camera, so that the shutter speed for flash (1/60th, 1/125th or a separate x setting) is set electronically. A light to indicate the flash is ready to fire may appear in the viewfinder as well.

(Through The Lens) TTL flash units have a further connection so that the light from the flash entering the lens is metered during the exposure and when the subject has had enough light, the flash stops. These models (on a limited range of SLRs) give very reliable exposure.

Bounce flash is a technique used to avoid red eyes and harsh shadows which can be created by a flash mounted on the camera. The flash is tilted up to the ceiling, and the light bounces off, softly diffused, to reach

the subject.

Some flashguns have bounce head, which tilt or swivel to allow this. You need a larger, more powerful gun to ensure results, and a computer sensor 'auto' flash removes the need to calculate light losses and distances. Many allow a choice of two or three working f-stops.

Tripods come in all weights and sizes, and their purpose is simply to hold the camera. They hold it in perfect alignment when composition is critical; they hold it in place when you want to leave it unattended, or include yourself in the picture; and they hold it steady, when your hand would be too shaky for long exposures or telephoto lenses. The usefulness of a tripod is directly related to its rigidity. Weight comes into this, but bulk is also important; thin, spindly legs are not much use

even if they are solid steel. You have to go into a dealer and try several types. Remember that a lightweight tripod which you are prepared to carry with you is far better than a superior heavy model which is too much trouble to use! The best models are made of light alloy, with large box-section legs and central columns with locking braces.

Lens-hoods are useful with many zooms and fast (wide maximum aperture) lenses. They prevent stray light entering the lens from just outside the picture area, and appearing as ghosting, misty flare or coloured hexagons across the image. Some modern lenses do not really need a hood, but makers still supply or recommend them because they also protect the front element from knocks.

Haze or skylight filters are another

Opposite page: accessories which you may need include flashguns, and a tripod. This one is a pocketable miniature version for travelling.

Above: a flashgun operating with through-the-lens exposure control can create interesting effects. In this case, the flashgun is hidden behind the book and the light is reflected from the pages on to the girl's face and background.
Photograph by *David Kilpatrick*.

optional extra, recommended to keep expensive lenses free from dust, moisture and scratches. A good dealer will probably offer you a filter with a new lens, and fit it in the shop. The best all-round type is a Haze or UV filter, made from almost colourless glass. Without affecting the picture in any other way, it removes excess blue from seascapes, snow scenes, landscapes and mountain views. If you take colour slides, a Skylight 1A or 1B filter is a better choice, as this is slightly stronger (tinted pink) and helps correct 'cold' skin tones on overcast days or in open shade. Apart from these basic filters, there are many other filter types to consider.

Yellow, orange and red filters are intended to change the way that black and white film records colours as tones. If you fit a coloured filter, then colours which are similar are recorded lighter and opposite colours are recorded darker.

The basic colours are 2× yellow, 4× orange and 8× red. These all do basically the same thing – they darken blue skies, make foliage lighter, and increase the contrast of outdoor scenes. The effect is progressively stronger as the colour is made deeper. A yellow filter gives a pleasant summery sky with white clouds just picked out; orange gives a richer effect; red can give dramatic near-black skies with bleached grass and pure white clouds. A green filter can improve landscapes and outdoor portraits, and a light blue filter tungsten light portraits indoors.

The *factors* given for the filters – 2×, 4×, 8× and so on – refer to how much to increase the exposure compared to a shot without the filter. They are used for flash and with hand-held metering; TTL metering takes filters into account and the film speed setting stays the same.

Colour filters

With colour film, the deep coloured filters for black and white would just give an overall coloured cast. Filters for colour are different. The most useful ones are the UV-Haze and Skylight 1A or 1B types you should leave fitted to your lenses all the time. For attractive skin tones, beach scenes, autumn landscapes and all shots when the sky is blue but the sun is behind a

cloud, a 'warm-up' filter Type 81A is worth trying.

Polarizers

Polarizing filters are extremely useful. Like polaroid sunglasses, they darken the sky when rotated, and cut down bright reflections. A polarizer is the best way to make skies a deeper blue in colour. Correctly rotated, it can eliminate reflections from plate glass windows, cut down glare from a wet street, let you see the grain of a polished wood table without surface sheen to hide it, or cut out reflections from a polished car. The effect of the polarizer can be judged through the lens.

Soft focus

Soft focus or diffusion filters are slightly misted or textured but otherwise clear. Without making the subject seem blurred, they take the hard edge off detail and soften it down. Portraits benefit particularly from soft focus.

Starbursts

Starburst and cross-screen filters are engraved so that when a light-source is included in a picture, a star or cross of light is seen radiating from it. This gives an effect making the light-source appear to 'shine', and can add life to otherwise rather static pictures.

Graduated filters

Some filters are clear in one half, with a gradual transition in the middle to become coloured or grey. These are graduated filters. They are intended for use mainly with colour film, to produce better skies. A blue graduated filter can 'put in' a sky on a dull day. Grey can deepen a pale blue sky. The other colours (a wide range) produce dramatic and vivid effects, which may or may not look realistic depending on the exact type.

A range of filters, all in a suitable thread to fit your main lenses, should include the basic protective UV or haze; black and white correction filters; soft focus or other special effects; graduated colour filters; and (**bottom**) a polarizer for use with both black and white and colour.

TAKING
PICTURES

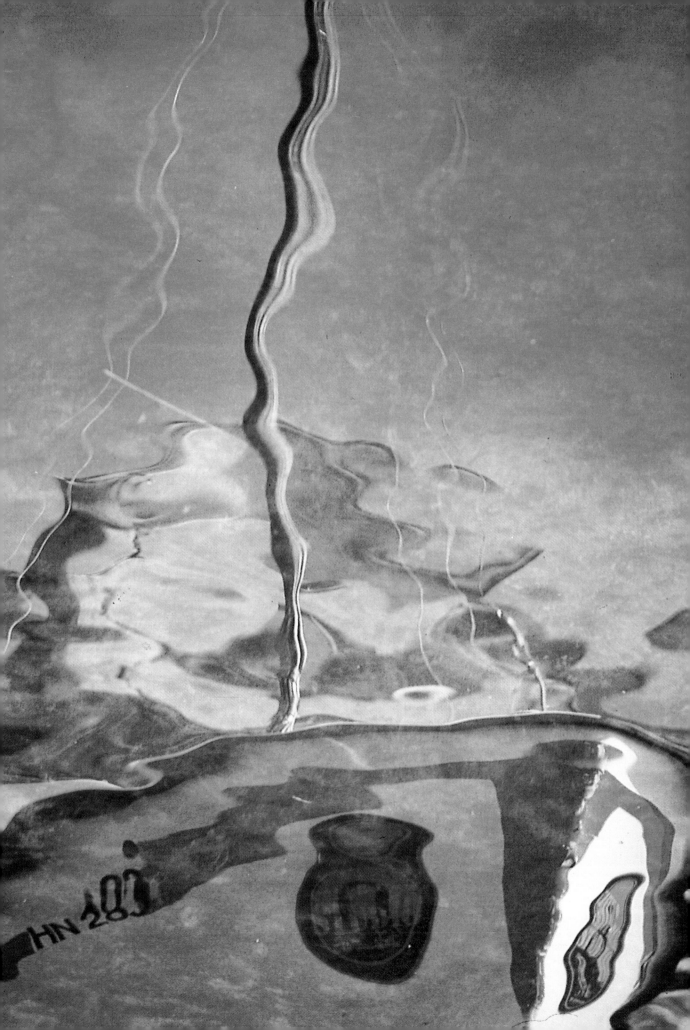

OUTDOOR PHOTOGRAPHY

Most pictures you take which are not of people will be of outdoor scenes. They may be landscapes, street scenes, buildings, sea-scapes, monuments or landmarks, gardens, almost anything – the kind of places you visit on holiday or at weekends. All pictures like this can be treated as one kind of shot, even though one picture might be of architecture and another one a beach scene.

When you are showing general outdoor shots like this to other people, remember that a place you have visited may not mean anything to them. You remember it, and the picture produces associations. For someone else, it either has to be a very good subject and picture to be interesting, or you have to include people.

It is a very good idea to include 'signs' in less recognisable scenes. No-one needs to be told where a shot of the Eiffel Tower was taken, but typical local costume, street names, shop signs and so on can help place otherwise anonymous shots and make them more interesting.

Conditions

Successful pictures have weather and other conditions which suit the subject. Take your family holiday group on the beach at the end of the holiday, when everyone is brown. A pallid one taken at the beginning might make an amusing comparison, but hardly a fair record on its own. Photograph picture-postcard scenes when it is sunny, streets when they are busy, beaches after the tide has cleaned them up, markets when they are in full swing, and so on.

Here are some examples of wrong conditions in outdoor pictures:

A fountain with the water turned off.

A woodland landscape in mid-winter without snow or sun.

Your garden when it hasn't been mown or weeded for weeks.

Bad conditions can provide amusing photographs. A windswept northern British beach with wrapped-up holidaymakers can be as interesting a shot as a sunny postcard view.

For professional photographers, wrong conditions can mean unusable pictures. For amateurs, they mean at the worst unsatisfactory pictures and at the best slightly amusing records. Keep taking pictures, wherever you go and whatever you do, but if things do not look right, do not go mad. You never know when a superb shot will appear and you will be glad you have plenty of shots left.

Lighting

Even when the sky is overcast, the light tends to come from the direction of the hidden sun. Overcast light is ideal for some subjects. For general scenes, it can be successful whenever the main subject is *vertical* or in a recessed position. There are some photographs, like a view of a building's north side, which are best taken on dull days. Other subjects may have deep areas of shadow, parts in sun and parts in shade, or look too harsh when the sun is out. Wait for the sun to go in if you can not return at a better time of day in sunlight.

Dull light is particularly unimpressive for seascapes, beach scenes, mountains, moorland, and modern street scenes. It is impossible to take good snow scenes in overcast light. Landscapes with large expanses of grass may look pleasant in soft, misty rain, but the brilliant green you expect from grass will be lost.

You often find superb lighting just after a rain-storm, with the clouds clearing and many elements improved by the depth of colour and shine given by the rain – wet foliage, wet rocks, wet sand or wet streets. The rainy-day effect is more in keeping with overcast light.

When the sun is out, beware of mist or 'flat' summer air which has no clarity. A combination of bright sun and clear air produces brilliant, crisp pictures. If there is too much haze results can be very flat. Shots during the day in warm countries often suffer from haze. The light colours of sand and white buildings will influence meter systems to give too little exposure, and dirty grey slides or prints will result.

'Keep the sun behind you', the old advice given to users of box cameras, is bad advice. Even on clear days, this kind of lighting is flat, revealing nothing of texture, shape or depth.

Opposite page: outdoor photography offers almost unlimited possibilities and can match the colour and style of studio work. Photography by *Peter Karry*.

Interesting lighting usually means not having the sun over your shoulder, and can often be discovered in situations where parts of the scene are in shade. This scene is strongly backlit and the camera itself was in deep shadow. Photograph by *David Kilpatrick*.

The best times for photography are from an hour after sunrise to an hour before sunset, missing out the two hours on either side of noon. The best general sunlight is semi-sidelighting; with the sun to your left or right, slightly behind you. This casts shadows sideways, including your own, so that it does not fall in the picture. One side of every vertical part of the subject will be brightly lit, with the other in shadow, and a gradual transition in the middle. This gives three-dimensional relief.

The sky, on a clear day, will be at its deepest blue when the sun is a few degrees behind you to one side. Where the light 'skims' surfaces like brickwork or bark, the texture will be picked out in sharp relief. Everything looks more solid, more colourful, and more attractive.

Although low sunlight often brings out the best in buildings and landscapes, there may be times when overhead sun does have benefits. Courtyards, alleys and small woodland clearings may only be well lit at mid-day. Sidelighting, around two hours before sunset or after sunrise, gives the best ground texture. But any nearby buildings or trees can easily cast long shadows which may fall on the subject, and you have to avoid extreme sun/shadow contrasts. Backlighting, where the sun is actually in front of you though not included in the shot, increases contrast by producing dark shadows facing the camera and bright highlights where the sun is either reflected off shiny surfaces, or shines through translucent ones.

Wet streets, the sea, rocks, grass, leaves in spring or autumn, subjects like boats or horses with simple strong silhouettes – all these look good in backlighting. Large bulky buildings, trucks, and anything with an unimpressive silhouette will look bad. Dry concrete or dust-roads both produce very poor pictures in backlight. Rivers in mountain valleys, islands offshore and cobbled roads make wonderful backlit scenes.

In backlight, the meter may indicate less exposure than you expect because of the bright sun coming directly towards you. Increase the exposure by 1 or 2 stops; it should be the same as the meter-reading taken with the sun

behind you. For silhouette effects, let the meter set its own exposure; for very light, airy effects, give one stop more than a normally lit scene indicates.

Focusing

Most outdoor scenes will be sufficiently far away for the depth of field to be unimportant. This means that almost any lens, and any lens aperture, may be used.

Where a scene contains a little more depth, focus either on the key subject in the view, or about one-third into the overall depth of the subject. If you decide to frame the picture by using a window, leaves, nearby buildings or some other foreground detail, use a small aperture to make this as sharp as possible. You should still set your focus on the view through the 'framing' foreground, and not on the foreground itself.

Often, a closed-down aperture to give enough depth of field to keep both framing and subject in focus

means too long an exposure time, and a tripod. In any normal landscape, there is usually some movement which will show if exposure times longer than 1/30th are used. Consider the idea of letting the foreground detail become completely blurred. Select a deliberately wide aperture instead, and use the foreground as an abstract frame. This works best when the foreground is a separate plane, like leaves hanging down in front of the lens, or a clump of flower sticking up. Natural forms work better than man-made or hard-edged shapes.

Composition

The idea of using a nearby element to frame a picture leads on to composition. Composition is most important when you are shooting outdoor scenes, because the whole balance of the picture depends on your chosen viewpoint, lens and final 'crop'. There is one old rule, the Rule of Thirds, which is easily mastered and improves pictures instantly. It is based

In some shots, a low camera position places important foreground detail very close to the lens. This calls for a small aperture to ensure depth of field, and the focus should be set about one-third of the way into the total depth of the scene – in this case, the wooden posts. Photograph by *David Kilpatrick.*

on the simple fact that the centre of the picture isn't the centre of visual interest:

This might seem nonsense. Surely your eye goes to the middle of the picture? Yes – but it doesn't stay there. The eye scans a picture, rather like a page of writing, starting at the top left and moving across and down. The centre is not a focus of attention. Points about one-third of the way from the edge of the picture are the strongest and most natural resting-places for attention.

So if you have a horizon, place it either:
ONE THIRD from the top of the frame
or
ONE THIRD from the bottom

If you have a vertical landmark like Nelson's Column place it one-third from either edge. The same would apply to a prominent tree, the most important building in a row, the main jet in a fountain, or to one of the 'clues' mentioned earlier which give your scene its identity. This type of composition naturally works best when there are different elements in a picture which can be placed by changing your viewpoint and distance.

Intersecting thirds provide the

strongest single points in pictures. There are four points, where two of the third-lines cross. These are good places for putting suns in sunsets, horses in fields, the building at the end or a pier, a hot-air balloon, a boat, and any other 'blob' rather than 'line' subjects.

Remember:

a) You use the central focusing aid in your camera's viewfinder to FOCUS, not to compose the shot. Reposition the main points of interest by deliberate composition *after* focusing.

b) Just by composing a shot with key elements on intersecting thirds, you help discover which are the key elements to focus on to begin with.

You can, of course, experiment with extremes of symmetry or total imbalance; dramatic perfect patterns centred exactly in the finder, or tiny subjects lost in a waste of unbroken landscape right up in one corner of a picture. The Rule of Thirds is simply a good starting-point and a key to 'safe' composition.

Composition effects

The Rule of Thirds would work, in theory, given a black dot, a line, and a blank sheet of paper. A typical scene is much more complicated, and there will be many elements in it. Together, they

Left: basic rules of composition help ensure a balanced picture. The tree, foreground area and sky all conform to the rule of thirds in their general positioning and porportions. Photograph by *David Kilpatrick.*

Opposite top: circles and fully enclosed curves contain the eye, and give a sense of tranquillity – even when fast motion is also implied. Photography by *Martin Lillicrap.*

Opposite bottom: repeated curves hold the viewer's eye, and lead it to the figure positioned exactly on an intersecting third. Photograph by *David Mark.*

form patterns, which may not be obvious to the eye but become clearer in pictures. The shape of the picture, and these hidden patterns, affects the way people see it.

Horizontal compositions (landscape format) tend to look tranquil and open.

Vertical compositions (portrait or upright format) look slightly more deliberate, active and uncertain, and also more closed-in.

Straight lines in a picture increase the sense of movement, formality, and structure. They also tend to divide it into competing sections.

Curves in a picture lead the eye round it, and do not divide it as much. Sharp, definite curves may have just as much movement as straight lines.

Ovals or any other enclosed, curve-formed shapes, attract the eye and try to contain it. They give a sense of tranquillity and harmony.

Triangles convey the idea of strongly conflicting forces, stress, and division.

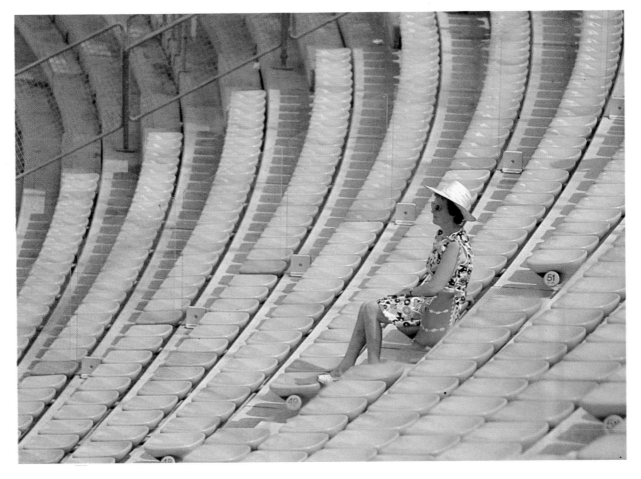

Diagonal lines, divisions or general directions convey movement or speed. A diagonal from bottom left to top right is seen by the eye as 'up' and a diagonal from top left to bottom right as 'down'.

Repeated shapes are ideal for showing depth of perspective, where they diminish in size, or for drawing attention to themselves; for example, any two things in one shot which resemble each other.

S-curves combine the harmony of oval forms with the structure of curved lines. The S-curve is one of the most compelling compositions, and holds visual attention. An S with a reduced top can be used convey depth – as with a road snaking into the distance. For the best effect the curve must start in the bottom left of the shot, like a real S. Reversed S shapes, or ones which read from the top, still work but not quite as well.

Concentric ovals or irregular curved shapes draw the eye to the centre. A good example might be trees, framing a lake, with an island in the middle.

Vertical lines make a shot look taller, more formal, more static but less stable.

Horizontal lines make a shot look longer, flatter, more natural, more stable and permanent.

Photographic composition is most clearly visible in black and white pictures. These shots by *David Kilpatrick* show some of the key points singly and in combination: **Opposite top, left:** an 'up' diagonal gives a strong sense of movement to a landscape. **Opposite top, right:** a vertical composition with vertical lines indicates formality in contrast to the random shapes and patterns within the picture. **Opposite bottom:** a strong perspective of repeated shapes combined with verticals enclosed in curves. **Top:** the diminishing size of the foreground rocks gives a powerful perspective and creates a hidden triangle pointing to the castle. **Bottom:** the path, buildings and movement of the subjects form a distinct S-curve composition snaking from bottom left to top right.

PORTRAITS

Portraits do not have to be formal; they are any pictures you take of people except the ones where a small group stands in front of a scene.

Photographers talk of *formal* portraits, meaning sit-down-and-look-at-the-camera pictures, with best shirt and tie and a plain background. *Informal* portraits are often truer to life, and can be taken quickly, in natural clothes, wherever you are. The subject is still aware of the camera, and you probably say 'look over here' and 'smile'.

Environmental portraits put the subject deliberately in front of a scene which relates to them. A farmer could be shown with a farm behind him, or a craftsman posing in his workshop. The pose is usually more formal than informal.

Candid portraits have the subject totally unaware of the camera. They are taken to show everything as it actually is, with the subject doing something or talking to someone, uninterrupted and certainly not looking at the lens.

Most of your own pictures are likely to be informal shots, with a few lucky candids when you can manage to use the camera with friends or family genuinely unaware. If you want to try formal portraiture, then you will need lighting equipment and backgrounds – almost your own studio. If you are lucky, outdoor backgrounds or convenient window-light and plain walls in your house may be suitable for apparently 'posed and lit' portraits, the only formal aspect being the sitter's response.

Right: a working environmental portrait puts the subject in a strong light from a single direct flash, while a 24mm wide-angle lens gives enough background detail to set the scene. Photograph by *David Kilpatrick*.

The important thing to remember in all portraits is that *faces* are interesting and *expressions* make them more so. People *doing* things are more interesting than people posing, and the *subject* must never be dominated by the *background*. As a rule, legs and feet are hardly ever vital to a portrait but the body and hands can be important.

There are some basic guidelines to portraiture which can be summed up neatly by remembering *three-quarters* as a key phrase. They are not absolute rules, but if followed they cut out many of the most common mistakes in everyday shots of people.

Three-quarters of the frame should be subject, whether it is a full face portrait, head and shoulders, or more distant shot.

Three-quarters is the best normal angle for a portrait, not dead-on to the face: both eyes visible, and the far cheek profile not broken by the nose, but only one ear shown. The body should also be at a slight angle to the camera, never photographed square-on, as this makes a person look very broad.

Three-quarters of a metre, 75cm, is the closest you should ever bring the camera for a shot of someone's face. Closer than this, and the result will look very distorted.

Three-quarter lighting is the best for portraits; light from slightly above and slightly to one side, so that about three-quarters of the face is lit and one-quarter faces away from the light direction.

Three-quarter length is the deepest picture you should take normally – cut off just above the knee, with men or women. Never include a knee and cut off just below it – this looks terrible. Cut off just below the waist, or just above the knee.

These simple rules, all based on remembering three-quarters as the key to good portraits, really do work.

There are a few other posing guidelines for extra polish. Never let your subject make *fists* with hands; ask for fingers to be spread. Never allow *crossed arms* unless you want the subject to look proud or defensive. Suggest a slight angle or tilt to the head to make composition more interesting. A table gives people a natural place to put hands. If not, see

Above: a three-quarter view of the face is combined here with unusual lighting and film to create a golden effect. Picture by *Len Harvey*.

Left: the same principles can be seen clearly applied in a totally different portrait by *David Kilpatrick*. Here, a lower viewpoint and instructions to the model to lift her chin and tilt her head emphasize neck length.

Above: *John Xavier* chose his angle and viewpoint carefully to give his subject appeal.

for *detail* as well as feeling.

If you want more attractive pictures of people, remember that your own eye-level is not necessarily the best viewpoint. Children should be photographed from their own level, or only very slightly above. Sit a child on a chair, or squat down to take pictures of children at play. Be very careful with wide-angle lenses, because at eye-level you end up looking down on the child from above if you are not careful. Pictures taken like this make toddlers look like gnomes with bulging foreheads.

Slightly *low* viewpoints make chins look bigger, foreheads smaller, ears flatter and noses both smaller and more retroussé. *High* viewpoints make faces triangular, with large foreheads and small chins, longer but slimmer noses, and more prominent ears.

High viewpoints also tend to dominate the sitter, so that they look smaller, and less aggressive; in women, more appealing to the male sense of domination. Low viewpoints look theatrical, heroic, and dominant because the sitter looks down on the camera and is made 'tall'. Not surprisingly, men like to be shot this way!

There are a few points to bear in mind about face types. Most of the time you will be best advised to correct, or avoid emphasizing, bad features. But sometimes the features are very much part of the character and may 'make' the shot. To please the sitter, shoot from the subject's own eye-level, which is by definition the view that they always see in the mirror.

To produce the right expression, it is often enough to say 'smile'. Bursts of laughter or grimaces produced by 'cheese' or 'knickers' may be too artificial. Hide a squeaky toy for children, or get mum to stand beside you and attract the offspring's attention. The best way to get good expressions is to take ten or more shots, so that there is a choice, and the initial few shots help the subject get over any hesitation about being photographed

if there is anything natural to hold; picked flowers, a handbag, a pen.

If someone does place their hand on a knee or a table, make sure the arm lies across the body and does not aim directly outwards towards the camera. When this happens it looks like a stub.

Watch out for wrinkled necks or double chins if you ask a subject to look round at you, or to look down. Photographing from slightly above eliminates double chins; lifting the chin or tilting the head cuts neck wrinkles. When taking portraits, look

Portrait lighting

Outdoor lighting for portraits is simple – anything but direct sunshine. Overcast days are ideal and give excellent colours, skin tones and no problems with half-closed eyes or harsh shadows. Wide apertures help blur the background.

If you are forced to take pictures outdoors in sunshine, then try asking your subject to move into the shade. Pick a spot where there is plenty of light reflected from nearby buildings or light-coloured ground. Green shade, under trees, can produce unpleasant colour casts and should be avoided.

Very attractive effects can be obtained by working in backlight. The sun should be facing the camera, directly above your portrait subject, well out of the picture, and not too high in the sky. Read your exposure from the face only – it will be about one stop more than a normal reading from the whole scene.

Backlight gives pleasant soft modelling on the face itself, which is fully in shadow, and the hair (especially with women and children) is picked out with a bright halo. To improve the results, ask the sitter to hold a newspaper or a sheet of white card (out of the shot, at waist level) which can reflect some extra light back into the face.

For a very light, summery effect give even more extra exposure than normal – two or three stops more than the normal reading.

Indoors, you may find you can sit your subject in a suitable corner of a room, and reflect sunshine coming in from a window to provide a soft, glowing light. Do not include any direct sun. Alternatively, ask your subject to sit or stand just next to a large window (not with direct sun) so that the soft light from the window falls on the face with almost the strength of the light outdoors. Shoot from one side, so that the curtain or wall is a backdrop, with perhaps a very small area of the shot including the window.

When the light is not good enough, try using the bounce flash to imitate natural window light. Aim your flashgun at a wall, or into the corner formed by the wall and ceiling, so that the light which bounces off this reflector surface aims at your subject. Flashguns which have automatic exposure and a check-light to indicate that there is enough light are most suitable.

Try natural tungsten light, with your subject next to a table-lamp, for a warm yellow glowing effect which can also be very flattering to complexions.

Above: a classic ambient light study by *Brian Skerrat* uses many of the key points – three-quarter length, hands, semi-profile face, backlighting and the use of uncorrected artificial light.

GLAMOUR AND FIGURE

Glamour and nude photography are extensions of portrait photography as far as most people are concerned. The exception is when the human body is treated as an abstract form, and photographed for its shape, texture and visual qualities.

It is fair to say that this level of work needs considerable grasp not only of photographic ideas, but also of artistic goals. By all means launch into the field if you have already studied art and know exactly what you are doing, or trying to do.

Glamour photography, as opposed to artistic figure work, is closer to home. You may have the opportunity to 'glamourize', or show in the best possible light, a wife, daughter, sister, friend, neighbour – almost anyone. There is no particular reason why this should be a male pursuit, as some of the best beauty and glamour photographers are women, with a finer eye for the detail of dress, hair and make-up than men.

There can be no real complaint, on moral or religious grounds, about glamour or nude photography handled in the right way. Deliberately salacious, revealing, undignified or perverted photographs have existed since the birth of photography; that bit of history goes way back before the camera, and nothing is likely to change it. Today you can have processed, without problems, any normal topless and decent nude photographs.

When trying to pose a shot deliberately, remember that the viewer will tend to look more at hands and feet than you do through the camera; they gain emphasis. People also look 50% wider in photographers than to the eye, or 50% shorter! The basic three-quarters guidelines mentioned for portraits apply just as much to figure and glamour photography.

For glamour portraits, all you need is a well-groomed, attractive made-up face with a winning look. Without the smile and the sparkle in the eyes, you

Below: glamour and figure photography can be just as abstract and creative as any other field, requiring the same sense of composition, lighting and colour as architectural or landscape work. In this shot, any girl with attractive hair could have been the model, even without professional training or make-up. The location is simply an empty beach in Tunisia, a few miles from tourist beaches. All photographs on this spread are by *Lorentz Gullachsen*.

end up with a dull picture, and part of the 'life' always comes from the photographer.

The secret behind impressive glamour portraits is eye-contact: the subject's eyes must look straight at the camera lens, so that they look out of the print straight at the viewer. Romantic or abstract figure studies should avoid this, and the model may look down, or at an imaginry sky. It can help to give a model a flower to hold, which deals with the problem of posing hands and what to look at in one go.

Unless you want your figure or nude photographs to be an amusing personal record of someone trying to be a model, which you wouldn't show to anyone else, pick your model very carefully. Good figure models are very slim, without exaggerated vital statistics, and some experience of training in ballet, gymnastics or good plain keep fit classes will help.

If you are seriously interested in exploring this field, you should be quite prepared to work with a model wearing a swimsuit or a leotard initially, to develop your ideas and see the first results. A photographer not prepared to do this almost certainly has exactly the wrong reasons for an interest in figure photography.

Posing and viewpoints

The guidelines given for portraits hold good for glamour work as well, but you may have to think hard about body-shapes. A high viewpoint for a shot of a girl is more likely to make her look appealing. The pose must be adjusted so that it does not give her a big head and short legs! Often this means a reclining, leaning, or angled pose; maybe even lying down. A low viewpoint can turn a healthy figure into a very strong, statuesque shot with the advantage that you may be able to set your subject against a clear blue sky. The problem can be that too close a camera position on this shot will give the subject big thighs – OK for a male bodybuilder but not a beauty queen!

Fashion photographers kneel down, bringing the camera to waist level, or position their models on a platform to make them look taller. They avoid oversizing legs, feet and rear ends by

using lenses of around 135–200mm and keeping a respectful distance.

Figure and glamour photographers, in contrast, sometimes use a stepladder to gain a high viewpoint and ask their model to drape casually over a chair. The stepladder probably only lifts the camera to a foot or so higher than normal, but it is more convenient than using a tall tripod and step-stool to stand on.

Never photograph a *figure* dead on. Always ask your model to stand at an angle to the camera, so that the body is viewed with a much thinner section. Avoid the squared-shoulders, 90° to the camera pose. One foot should be brought forward, and most 'weight'

Below left: a high viewpoint allows a simple composition with the model laying down, and open shade provides smooth lighting.

Below right: a low viewpoint, a three-quarter angle to the girl's figure combine with a polarizing filter for impact.

Bottom: a combination of warm evening sunshine colours and body-make-up matched to the colour of jewellery and rocks, in a simple composition.

put on the leg furthest from the camera when standing. When your model sits or kneels, she should put all her weight on the hidden or furthest leg. This is also important with squatting and kneeling poses where the thigh of the leg bearing the weight will bulge. An arm put out to help balance may solve this, but watch out for lumpy upper arm muscles near the shoulder – a simple twisting of the hand can eliminate this. In time you recognise faults before they happen and give models instructions which avoid problems.

Always ask your model to stretch or straighten her neck, and widen her eyes. A relaxed pose tends to include a dropped head position, often with neck wrinkles, and rather 'dull' eyes. The slightly overworked tummy in/chest out/shoulders back/head up/right leg forward-a-bit routine which many experienced glamour and figure photographers use is not just an attempt to make limited assets look larger. It introduces some stretch and tension into a static pose, much in the same way a dancer has to create these particular aesthetic qualities.

Movement is probably a better solution; photograph your subject actually walking, running, jumping or dancing. Many fashion photographers do this all the time. It eliminates the 'slump' of a normal standing pose without all the cajoling and apparently repetitive instructions. To do this well, you need practise combined with the some technical skill. A motor driven camera helps catch the best moment out of five or six possible shots, and flash can freeze the action.

These tips don't just apply to fashion and glamour work or nude and figure photography. They are useful when you are simply photographing a friend on the beach on holiday, because if you avoid the 'dead' and 'flat on' poses, pick your viewpoint, and adjust your subject's poise for a better effect you will create a far more flattering picture. This certainly works as well with teenage boys, grannies and workmates as it does with calendar models. Everyone looks better with a bit of deliberate poise and composure.

Below: the psychology of a glamour shot depends on many things. In this picture by *David Kilpatrick*, a high viewpoint and reclining model are both used. Direct eye contact, and warm lighting add to the effect. The shot was produced using a fur fabric background and two flashguns, with the model on the floor, shooting with a 50mm lens from a step-stool.

Lighting for glamour

If you have your model, your location and your equipment ready the remaining factor to make or break the results will be the quality of light. The secret is *soft* lighting. Never let direct sunlight strike the face or skin or your model unless you are very sure of perfect make-up and flawless complexion. In soft light, most people can be made to look pleasant.

Backlight involves having your camera aiming towards the sun and the model facing you. The exposure should be read carefully from the shadow area, and you must not allow odd rays of sun to strike across the model's shoulders and pick out highlights. The background will probably be very bright and the overall effect sunny.

Open shade means that you take your model on to the shadow side of the street, out of the sunshine, and shoot by the light reflected into the shaded area from nearby buildings or ground. The quality obtained is often

most flattering. Beware colour casts – these are caused if the sunlight is reflected off a green lawn, a blue building and so on. Colour casts from warm tones like sand, white or cream buildings and so on are totally acceptable. You can make your own neutral reflected light by positioning an old sheet in the sun to bounce light back into a shady area. You can even make the shaded area itself by using your car, tent fabric, or a similar portable obstruction.

As a rule, morning and evening light outdoors works better for glamour shots than mid-day sun. Flash should either be direct, on the camera, or set up in a proper studio with full control. Direct flash is more flattering than many photographers think. Bounce flash, on the other hand, is unflattering for work involving face and figure (clothed or otherwise) because the direction of the light, from the ceiling in front of the model, causes poor modelling and also falls off in intensity around the waist and legs.

Above left: low sunshine in the early morning or late evening is the best form of direct lighting, enhancing skin tones. Photograph by *Lorentz Gullachsen*.

Above right: the soft lighting from an overcast day in England provided a moody but natural atmosphere for this outdoor shot by *Roger Newman*, taken using a 250mm mirror lens.

STILL LIFE

Still life conjures up unfair images of bowls of fruit and jugs with loaves. Anything which you can study through the camera for its shape, colour, and form may be classed as still life unless it gets up and walks off.

Still life in your garden could include old plant-pots, a pair of gloves in a shed, or a plastic gnome. Still life in the house could be a selection of crystal glass, a favourite heirloom, something the kids made at school, fruit, the bathroom windowsill or a box of spare buttons.

The great still-life painters excluded everything from their paintings which was unwanted. The backgrounds tended to be vague, the table-tops on which things were placed were marble or wood; neutral, natural textures. Simplification and exclusion are the secrets of photographic still life, too. Outdoors, come in as close as you can. It is better to crop the subject itself a little, rather than include too much surrounding space. Look for colours and textures.

Here's a tip. Instead of focusing your camera with the lens starting on infinity, set the focusing to the closest possible distance. Now move in, until the shot is sharp. If you are too close, move back out again as you refocus. The easiest still life shots to start with are *flat* ones, like an old glove lying on the ground, or a pen lying on a page of a diary. You can use wider apertures, without worrying about tripods, as long as you keep the camera parallel to the subject plane. Indoors, and later on, you may want to shoot a still life from a side view, with considerable depth. Use a tripod. There is little point in doing a still life shot without good technical quality.

Colour films are so good today that you can produce superbly vivid images easily. Try strong colour contrasts like a bright red pepper (polish it first) on a green plate. Use your eyes every day – interesting small arrangements of ordinary things may be picked out by existing light, and make unexpectedly good photographs.

Below: one approach to a still life with wine in a glass as the subject, showing how new ideas make still life far from traditional. Photographed with a 20mm lens, illuminated perspex sheet and pegboard by *Richard Bradbury*. **Opposite bottom:** given the same lighting, and the same choice of camera equipment, *Andreas Vogt* set up a classical still life with grapes, bread and cheese and shot it on a 75–150mm zoom lens.

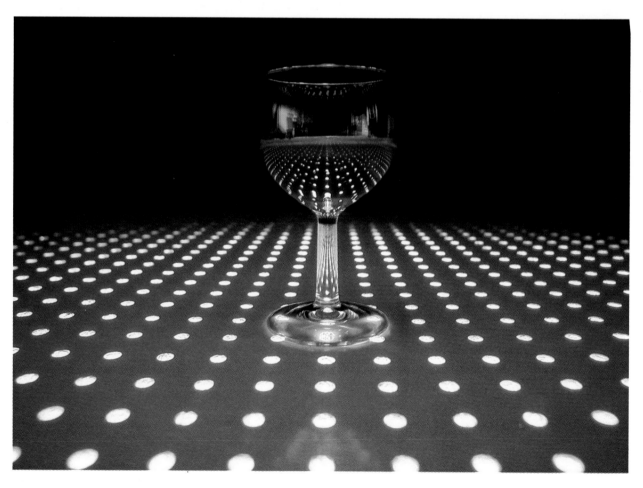

Lighting is very important in still life shots. At first, just look out for the effects of sunlight through windows. You may find that when the glass is covered in condensation, old and dusty in a garden shed, or curtained with a net the quality of direct sunshine on a group of objects is much improved. A bowl of fruit placed in the diffused patch of light from a net-curtained window can look very colourful and three-dimensional, but also very rounded and glossy.

The stage after this is to make your own lighting conditions – a home 'studio' – by obtaining some frosted plastic sheet, net curtain or tracing foil and pinning over a window. You can then play around with the position of chosen subjects. To improve the light quality, use medium sized mirror tiles for direct reflection or insulating tiles of white polystyrene foam for general reflection. You will be surprised how much difference these make and how you can build your own 'lighting' in this way.

David Mark found this still life composition in a window, and photographed it without the need to rearrange or light the subject, using a hand-held camera and 50mm lens.

Contrasts in still life approaches.
Opposite page: a studio study of pasta. Notice how the careful use of lighting has been used to bring out the different textures of the pasta.

Below left: a 'found' still life in a cathedral, by *Richard Bradbury* (35mm lens). **Lower left:** a domestic flash still life by *John Rawlings* (50mm macro lens). **Right:** a contrived and planned studio still life by *Richard Bradbury* (16mm fisheye lens with built-in yellow filter).

Outdoors, then, you keep an eye open for unusual still life subjects in good lighting. Indoors, you try to arrange them. After a while you can bring the whole thing into existence yourself, picking up an interesting item in a junk shop or buying some particularly good fruit. Natural effects can be planned and subjects can be 'planted' and allowed to weather, like an old axe deliberately lodged in a tree-stump with a view to shooting it covered in frost the next morning.

If you are short of ideas like this, try craft fairs or hobby groups. Flower arrangers can create very interesting texture and colour studies; woodturners, silversmiths, potters and the like will often be delighted to let your photograph their work. You will find in time that glassware and polished metal cause the biggest problems, and whole books have been written about solving them! It is a great challenge to take up. Always use the depth of field preview (if fitted to your SLR camera) to check effects with these subjects.

Equipment for still life can be simple; an ordinary good 35mm SLR with a standard 50mm lens is all that you need. An 85mm or 100mm lens produces better perspective for groups of objects and allows you to cut out unwanted background. A close-focusing type like a 90mm macro lens is even better, because still life subjects can be very small indeed – jewellery, items like pins or watch mechanisms, and so on.

A tabletop tripod or camera clamp is useful because you can not always get a full sized tripod into the right place to shoot a still life subject you have found. Close-up lens attachments and filters which diffuse the outer edge of the picture but leave the centre sharp are also an asset for some subjects.

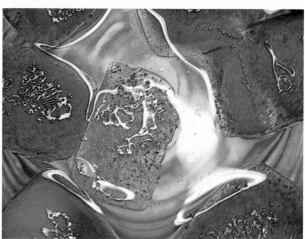

CLOSE-UPS

Once you come closer than the 45cm or so which most SLR standard lenses will focus to, you need some additional accessories to ensure sharp results. It is not enough to rely on depth of field.

The simplest accessory is the *close-up lens*. This is a weak magnifying glass, optically corrected, which screws into the front thread of your standard lens. They are available in three strengths, which allow you to focus down to less than 10cm. Some very powerful so-called 'macro' close-up lenses are inexpensive, need no special techniques in use, and fit any type of SLR lens.

A set of *extension tubes* will do much the same, allowing shots as close as 10cm with a 500mm lens, but with better sharpness. The tubes fit between the SLR body and the lens. Focusing and metering remain just as normal, but if you use flash there is a table to refer to, supplied with the tubes, to adjust the aperture you set.

Depth of field, as you see when looking through the tubes and 50mm lens, is very limited. A slight movement of subject of camera, and focus is lost entirely. For best results, you have to be careful about the depth of subject included, and use a small aperture like f11 or f16 with a tripod or flash.

Bellows are longer than extension tubes, and fit in the same way. Only

Opposite: the world of close-ups reveals more than the eye ever sees – by *J. Cummings*.
Below left: a tiny greenfly completes a composition with a poppy stem, by *Mike Travers*.
Below: *Duncan McEwan* stalked this dragonfly in its natural Scottish habitat with a 90mm macro lens.

the best ones transmit lens functions to the camera so that metering and aperture controls work automatically; lower cost bellows units need manual operation of the aperture.

There are various accessories made for bellows units, like slide copiers, rigid stands for photographing flat specimens, rails to mount the whole camera and bellows on a tripod, and special lenses. They are only of interest to the advanced worker, as all extreme close-up techniques require great care. Simple slide copying devices which do not need bellows, close-up lenses and extension tubes will tackle most of the shots an SLR owner is likely to want.

Slide copiers

For less than the cost of a lens, you can buy a slide copier with its own built-in optical system. The slide is inserted into a slot at one end, and the copier fits on to the SLR in place of the lens. Aiming at the sun or bright sky, there is no need to focus. With one of these, you can make colour or black and white negatives from your slides, for prints.

Viewfinder attachments

When you do close-ups, you may end up with the camera close to the ground, and be unable to get your eye up to the finder. A right-angle viewfinder attachment solves the problem, attaching to the eye-piece. You look down into a tube and see the image as normal. Some cheaper models show it reversed left to right, which can be confusing.

For very accurate focusing, magnifying attachments fit in the same way. You can not see the whole screen through these, but the central focusing aid is enlarged so that very fine adjustments can be made.

Lenses and uses

Different lenses you already own may alter the way you tackle close-ups. Extension tubes, for example, can be used on a zoom lens but the zoom

Right: by keeping the camera parallel to a flat subject and using a fast shutter with a wide aperture, *Duncan McEwan* eliminated any camera shake or subject movement in this 90mm macro lens shot.

action will no longer work properly. As you zoom, the image will go out of focus. Zoom lens owners are much better off with the close-up lenses which simply fit the front thread of the zoom, and change the focus to a closer point while retaining all the normal focus and zoom actions of the lens. The longer the lens, within reasonable limits, the better it will prove for outdoor close-up work. With a normal 50mm lens, you may have to go so close to a flower that your own shadow falls over it. Insects take flight because you come within their range of sharp vision. A 200mm lens fitted with a suitable close-up attachment will let you take the same picture from four times the distance, so your own shadow and presence do not matter as much.

Camera shake is a major problem with close-ups. Extension tubes and close-focusing using purpose made macro lenses both involve a considerable loss of light; at 1:1, or life size image on the film, a 'normal' shutter speed of 1/125 has to be extended to 1/30. Using close-up lenses does *not* involve this loss of light, though they are optically slightly inferior. In most cases, the macro settings of zooms are also free from any light loss. So in practical working terms you may get superior pictures from these 'cheap' and supposedly inferior methods.

Subject shake is also visible when you try to take a close-up of a flower in the breeze. At very close distances, the subject can seem to be buffeted about in a gale. Pick still, calm days for close-up shots. This movement can be frozen while at the same time ensuring sharp focus in depth if you use an electronic flash on the camera, combining a daylight exposure with flash. Special close-up ringflashes which surround the lens for shadow-free illumination are made just for this.

Ordinary camera-top flashguns can be unsuitable because when the lens is only two or three inches from a subject, the flashgun is six or nine inches above it and much further away. The subject will probably only catch the very edge of the light from the flash. An extension cord to allow you to remove the flash from the camera and hold it to one side of the

subject will make sure you aim the flash at the area being photographed, and also give better modelling and textural rendering as the flash will no longer be 'flat' on.

For all these aspects of close-up work, whether indoors with a carefully set-up specimen and a tripod or outdoors on your hand and knees stalking bugs, an SLR camera with through-the-lens off-the-film flash exposure is a great advantage. Such a camera will probably also combined the natural daylight with the flash in the correct proportion, compensate for any extension or close focusing devices used, and give precise exposure without calculations or trial and error.

Below: close-ups can be made at home (upper picture) with unexpected subject-matter like a broken windscreen lit using coloured flash. Photograph by *Dr Keith Hewitt*. **Lower picture:** a wide aperture, an oblique angle and a lens used beyond its normal recommended close focusing range produced an interesting effect with water on rose-petals for *Peter Karry*.

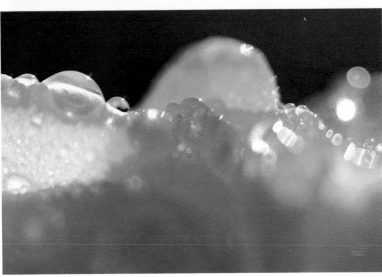

ACTION SHOTS

There are two basic approaches to action. You can aim for frozen movement, so that every detail is sharp whatever speed the subject was travelling; or you can aim for an impression of speed, which may be totally blurred and streaked although the subject is still recognisable. There are stages in between, and one of the best action effects happens when the subject itself is 'frozen' but the background is motion-streaked.

Panning

Panning, the act of following a moving subject with the camera, is the most important technique to learn. You must avoid *centering* the subject on your viewfinder focusing aid as you follow it, which always puts the subject bang in the centre of the picture. The second skill to master is the *follow through*, continuing the pan after the shot is taken. You should press the shutter smoothly, and never stop the panning movement. The finder blacks out for a moment when you fire. Try to ignore this. Practice

first, without winding on, to get the feel right.

There are some exceptions to the rules of panning. If you are using a camera which has auto-focusing based on a reading taken from the central viewfinder target, then you must try your best to ensure that the subject *is* centered up all the time and does not leave the target rectangle. If you waver, and the auto focus 'looks' at a different distance, it will probably be delayed and have another series of readings to take before catching up again with the subject.

Secondly, if you are taking pictures for ordinary colour enprints from negatives, it is much better to keep the subject well in the centre of the picture and then crop the print later on to balance the composition. This is the best way to tackle action panning with a one-touch type camera using an optical viewfinder, which may not be as clear as an SLR finder for following the subject. It is better to make sure you include all your subject, rather too centrally, than to cut part off by trying

Opposite: the power of a long telephoto lens compresses two motorcross riders banking round the track in this 300mm tele shot by *Alan Beastall.*

Below: a wide-angle used from a ground level viewpoint throws BMX riders into relief against the sky. Photograph by *Ian Buckden.*

for a creative composition.

Even with a SLR, long exposures during a pan can be difficult to follow through, because the finder stays blank for too long. Keep your other eye open, and follow the subject this way, swinging from the hip rather than moving your head.

Focusing

It is almost impossible to focus on any moving subject reliably, whether you are panning or not. The latest autofocus SLRs are far better than the human eye, brain and hand at performing this task. If you don't own one, then the answer is to pre-focus. The secret is simple; in most sports or displays, each participant passes the same point. Set your focus first, on a bend in the track, a marker post, a hurdle or some other clear reference.

Ignoring the fact that the picture will start out of focus, pick up your intended subject and pan with it. As it approaches the pre-focus point, it gets sharper. Do not try to judge the sharpness, or adjust your pre-set focus. Release just before it reaches the reference point and your natural delay in reflexes will give correct timing.

Slow speed pan

To give an impression of movement, use the slow speed pan technique with any subject moving across your field of view at a smooth pace. If you select a shutter speed like 1/1000, the background and subject should be equally sharp. At a speed like 1/125, the background will show a slight blur, and the subject will still be sharp. At a speed like 1/30 the background will probably be streaked, giving a clear impression of movement, and the subject may have some unsharp areas (spokes or hubs or wheels, for example).

For a totally fluid, impressionistic result, use speeds like 1/8 or even 1/2, with the necessary small apertures.

Deliberate motion blur

If shot with the camera static on a tripod, so that the background is sharp but the subject blurred, the result will show the track of the subject's motion. This only works well with a few subjects, and you have to experiment. Rowing eights and floodlit gymnastics both make good subjects for this technique.

In general terms any linear or regular motion may work, particularly if some element of the subject stays static or the movement passes repeatedly through one point. Light subjects against darker backgrounds record properly; dark subjects like birds against bright backgrounds like the sky are wiped out, and fail to record on the film. The ideal kind of subject would be a spotlit trapeze artist.

Flash and motion

Electronic flash freezes action very effectively, and can have a duration so short that even the droplets of sweat punched from a boxer's face are frozen in mid-air. More often than not, the subject is too far away to allow flash shooting.

Combined natural light and flash gives the best of both worlds – a fluid blur, with a sharp partial exposure picking out the subject at one moment in the action. Simply use your flash with a long shutter speed like 1 second in low light, giving about half a stop less exposure than normal.

Opposite top: a slow speed pan shot by *Leslie Fletcher* gives a strong impression of fast movement.

Below: slow speed with electronic flash sets a sharp subject against a blurred background. Photography by *David Kilpatrick*.

Motor drives

Any of these techniques – fast shutter speed, pan, slow speed pan, motion blur and flash – can be used with an auto-winder attachment in single frame mode, where the winder simply advances the film after you take your finger off the shutter.

Some auto-winders and motor-drives only operate in *continuous* mode, which means that as long as you keep your finger pressed, the camera fires repeatedly. With long exposures, this can be unsatisfactory as the cameras can fire at the wrong moment. Flash units may not be able to recycle fast enough to keep up with the drive. So when using motor drives, make sure you either use a fast shutter speed or a special fast charging flash for continuous frame sequences. The speed of a typical small winder is between 1.5 and 2.5 frames per second, whether built in to the camera or attached separately. A full motor drive gives from 3 to 6 frames per second.

Motor wind operation is invaluable in sports and action work where the total sequence of movement is continuous and too rapid for manual firing. This applies in motor sports,

water sports like sailing or surfing, 'linear' actions like diving or 'unbroken' actions like dancing. Here, so many different possible shots occur so quickly that it is best to use the motordrive in bursts of five or six frames as you think the general flow is reaching a peak.

In other sports, the winder should not be used for 'machine gun bursts', because you may miss the one critical moment and get all the other shots instead. Examples here would include a pole-vaulter at the top of the jump, a stunt motorcyclist going through a hoop of fire, or a pair of circus artistes joining hands in a mid-air trapeze act.

Above left: a slow speed exposure with a hand-held camera allows the subject motion to record naturally in this shot by *M. Gardner*.

Above right: *Chris Davis* operated the zoom action of his lens during a 1/15th of a second exposure of a bowls player in action.

81

Viewpoints and lenses

So many action pictures are taken from standard vantage-points that they all look alike – they have the compressed, perspective-free appearance of shots from a long telephoto lens. Action can be made more dynamic and immediate by getting very close to the subject and using a wide-angle. With some sports this is out of the question, but most SLR systems do accept special remote triggers using infra-red cordless signals so that a motordrive camera can be fired from the sidelines, but hidden near the action.

With other sports, including most home-grown ones, it is easier to get in close. A low viewpoint turns even a small jump of a foot or two off the ground into enough clearance to show a stunt bicycle rider 'airborne'. You may be able to get your subject to co-operate and very careful go through an action with you and the camera positioned midstream. This makes action work exciting even in a school or home environment.

Top: with a 16mm fisheye lens, a motordrive and a remote infra-red trigger, *David Kilpatrick* was able to bury a camera below a jump for this unusual viewpoint.
Above: *M. Grice* shot this sailboarder from a very close angle.

WILDLIFE

Wildlife has considerable appeal as a photographic subject if you have the resources and patience, and most people can try photographing garden birds, park squirrels, or deer on country estates. Shyness is the biggest problem to overcome: a combination of quiet behaviour, tempting the subject with food, and a telephoto or zoom lens may be needed. A focal length of 200mm will be enough for most purposes, but a 500mm mirror lens is a favourite optic with most serious wildlife photographers because of its extra 'pulling power'.

The technique of pre-focusing, as with action shots, is useful. Set your focus on a known likely landing-point; a bait of nuts for a squirrel, or a nest with young where a bird will land. Pick up the subject before it arrives, and follow it, rather like panning though less predictable. Do not adjust the focus; press the shutter a fraction before the pre-set point is reached. With a tripod, you do not even need to have your eye to the camera. Just watch the subject and when it reaches the area you have already framed up, fire the shutter.

Special precautions may be needed to avoid frightening subjects, or to fit in with their natural habits. Keeping the camera indoors or inside your car can help. Many animals are now used to motorists, and walk round freely near cars, but would move off if you opened the door to get out. An open window can be used to attach a special 'camera clamp' with a ball and socket head, turning the car into a tripod as well as a hide. This technique is not recommended in safari parks where open windows can be a hazard.

The kind of remote infra-red trigger and motordrive kit so useful in sports and action shots can also help you catch small, shy animals from very close positions. The camera is set up at the start of the day near a feeding table, as discreetly as possible. It may take hours for birds or small animals to get used to it, but eventually you can fire the shutter from your armchair. The latest autofocus SLRs are ideal for this type of shot because

Below: flash gives a brilliant and sharp rendering of lemurs in a zoo. Normal flash units do not harm animals even if they are nocturnal. Photograph by *Donald Packman.*

they also cope with different subject positions.

At night, the infra-red flash focusing system of the Minolta 7000 and Polaroid 600 series cameras will produce perfectly sharp pictures of wildlife when the human eye can not see it. There are several special tripping devices available which contact to cameras in the same way as the remote trigger kits, and these respond to an animal breaking a light beam or just to vibration. They are not expensive, and they bring professional wildlife photography techniques within reach of many SLR system owners.

In zoos

Modern zoos are not always a series of cages, and some wildlife photographers use the natural environments set up for animals to secure apparently realistic shots. For this type of work, you need a long lens of around 200–300mm and perhaps a 500mm mirror lens. Zoo compounds prevent the animals from going too far from visitors unless it retires to sleep, so extreme lengths are hardly ever necessary and an ordinary 70–210mm zoom will cover most shots.

To lose the wire from your shots, place the lens very carefully right up to the wire mesh itself, and use a wide aperture like f5.6 or f4. This will throw the mesh so far out of focus that it 'disappears' in the shot. Sometimes,

the mesh is just wide enough to allow the lens to be placed so that no wire obstructs the view. Be careful about apertures. As you normally view through your SLR at full aperture, you may not see wire mesh when it will appear in any shot taken at the final working aperture. Use the depth-of-field stop down preview.

Careful selection of viewpoints and close cropping of the subject, to remove as much evidence of man-made surroundings as possible, can produce very realistic images in zoos. The quality of light may give away the fact that this is London and not Kenya, and the type of meat being eaten, or the type of grass might tip off any expert instantly. If this matters, then you must take your skills and your camera on safari and look for the real thing.

Zoo vs safari. **Below:** a special camera viewpoint in Chester Zoo enabled *David Kilpatrick* to shoot this lioness feeding with a zoom set at 200mm, but the meal and the grass give the location away. **Right:** *Bruce Davidson* shot his leopard and prey in their natural surroundings in Kenya.

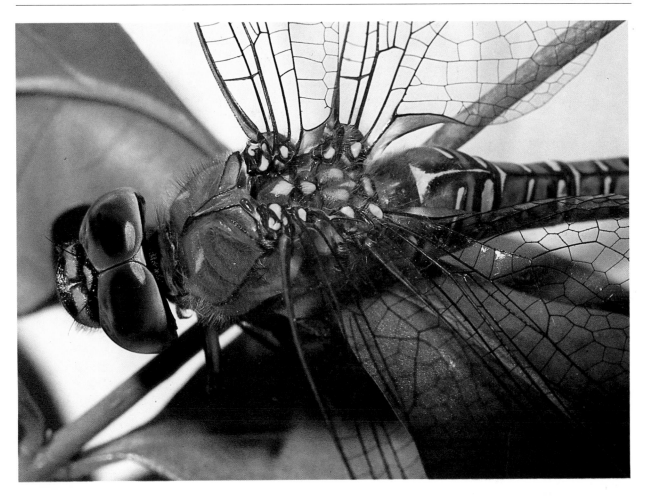

Small subjects

'Wildlife' may not seem the right title to use for very small mammals and insects, and at this level you tend to be more involved with the close-up aspects than the environmental ones.

At home, you can make a photographic vivarium to hold any small mammals or reptiles. This consists of a normal aquarium in design, but fitted with an extra compartment which is deliberately very narrow. The animal is confined within a minimum acceptable depth (say 2.5–5 cm for a mouse) and able to run freely backwards and forwards in this glass 'track'.

The camera can be positioned to keep this distance in focus, and you then wait for the right moment and position of the subject. When photographing through glass, make sure you do not use flash on the camera – it will reflect back and probably obscure most of the image with a large bright glare.

Above: the exquisite detail of an insect in extreme close-up, shot by *Dennis Turner* with a macro lens and Kodachrome film. **Below:** the appeal of a different kind of small subject – young creatures always make good pictures. Photograph by *Ian Gray*.

ARCHITECTURAL PHOTOGRAPHY

For those with an interest in buildings, architectural photography offers a way of recording places visited and showing specific points to others. The field covers exteriors, interiors, and details.

A tripod is essential, and a choice of the standard lens, one or two good wide-angles, and telephotos of 100 and 200mm is needed. Lights or flash equipment are not normally used, as the quality of light inside a building is part of the architect's intention, and you should try to incorporate this into pictures by using natural light only.

Good architectural pictures either have perfect geometry, with all vertical lines shown as perfectly upright and parallel in the picture, or an acceptable balance with natural perspective. This means that lines can be shown converging, in a natural way, using a balanced composition to cut out any impression of the building falling over.

Architectural balance. **Below left:** dead centred convergence by *Gordon Wigens*; **Top right:** balanced asymmetry from *S Lyttle*. **Lower right:** perfect pendiculars from *David Mark*.

Verticals

Good parallel verticals can be achieved two ways. You must keep the camera's film plane as closely aligned to vertical itself as possible – as if the top of the camera had a spirit level. If you stand on a elevation, around the same height as the middle of a building, then you can be as close as you like and still achieve this. If you have to stand on the ground, then the further away you can get with a long focus lens, the less you will have to tilt the camera upwards.

This does have the effect of making the building look rather solid and blocky, like a child's drawing, without much natural perspective. You may also find obstructions like people or trees get in the way. Very often a wide-angle picture taken from nearer the subject will convey a better impression of form and scale – so how do you solve the converging verticals? *Cropping* a picture composed with a large area of empty foreground is one solution; building in the top of the frame, concrete in the bottom . . . trim the print to remove the concrete!

This may not be a reasonable solution if you want your picture to be a full size print or an uncropped slide. Instead, look for subject-matter in the foreground to fill the otherwise blank area. It could be a well maintained pathway leading to the building, a flower bed, street furniture, or a wall. Even a slight elevation obtained by standing on a seat or on a rigid camera case you afford enough leeway to improve such a composition.

It is possible to correct converging verticals in two ways if you are forced to accept them in the picture through constraints of position and lens angle. The first method is to use a darkroom and enlarger, making a print, with the printing paper at an angle to the enlarger in a special set-up which exactly counteracts the original fault. This is a fairly skilled job. If you have no darkroom, but own a close-up lens or macro zoom, you can have a print made from your original shot and copy it with the print at an angle to the camera. This does exactly the same thing rather more crudely.

Perspective control

For serious architectural photographers, there are special lenses made for 35mm SLRs and called 'perspective control' (PC) or 'shift' lenses. They are usually available in focal lengths of 35mm (medium wide angle), 28mm (wide angle) and 24mm (super-wide angle). You must expect to pay around three times the price of a similar normal lens.

A 'PC' lens has a control which allows the lens itself to move off-centre from the film – up or down, or sideways, on the front of the camera. As you operate the control, you see the

Top: to keep verticals straight in a normal view, *Raymond Lea* used the reflections in the lake to balance the composition and allow a level camera angle with a 35mm compact one-touch.

Above: a distant viewpoint from a slight elevation, using a 75–150mm zoom lens set at 150mm, enabled *David Kilpatrick* to record Chatsworth house with minimal perspective and dead vertical lines.

Above: the effect of using a 35mm perspective control lens. The upper picture has no movements used, but the camera is angled upwards. The lower version has the camera held level, with a rise movement applied to the lens. Both photographs taken on a 35mm CA Rokkor lens by *John Hannavy.*

image-area viewed shift. By aligning the camera vertically, then moving the lens upwards (called 'using a rising front movement') you can bring a tall building into the field of view without any leaning verticals, from a close viewpoint. The effect is often dramatic because the building would not normally be seen 'correctly' from so close up. On subjects which would almost be acceptable with a normal lens, the PC lens simply enables absolute perfection.

Some PC lenses are very simple, with a single control and the ability to rotate the whole unit so that this

control applies to any direction of 'shift'. Others have a horizontal and vertical scale with two adjustments. The most expensive types have other features which allow the plane of focus to be altered, but this is a very specialized control not normally needed for architectural work and applied more to studio and creative close-up photography.

Deliberate drama

Having said that the aim of most architectural photography is a correct, accurate rendering there is also a strong school supporting shots which go the other way, where buildings crowd in and converge dramatically to a deep blue sky with sunbursts and acres of glass. This approach works superbly with extreme wide-angle lenses of around 17mm to 21mm, in circumstances where no ordinary technique can ever correct verticals. The skyscraper canyons of modern cities are best tackled either in this way, or from a great distance with a powerful telephoto.

Interiors

In cathedrals and churches, the floor itself is often so interesting that it can occupy half the picture, eliminating the need for special measures to keep the columns and windows straight. The ceiling, on the other hand, is accepted as correct if you simply angle the camera up and shoot. It is most important to balance any composition with formal design so that it does not appear to lean.

Modern rooms may have large areas of fluorescent lighting and these give two problems – firstly, the colour shows as green on most films, and the ceiling is excessively bright. You should fit a special 'FL-D' fluorescent to daylight colour conversion filter on the camera, avoid including too much ceiling, or if necessary shoot with the ceiling lights turned off. Always base your exposure reading on the floor even if this seems very dark. A flashgun on the camera helps but be careful not to aim at a window which might show a strong reflection of the flash. Use your eyes to spot this when you fire the shutter.

Very dark interiors, like cellars and old castles, may seem beyond the range of the film. There may be very bright, small windows which fool your eye and make the whole area seem too contrasty and black to photograph. Under these conditions, mount the camera on a tripod and use automatic exposure if you can, setting any available 'over-ride' to +1 and +2 steps. It pays to bracket the exposure. When the pictures are returned you may be surprised at how much colour and detail the camera picks out in apparently gloomy areas.

Detail shots are interesting when you compile a record of a building. For these, use your tripod and good medium telephoto lens – avoid zooms, because they may distort straight lines too much. Look for the decoration at the head of columns, for carvings, windows, cornices, fireplaces, butresses, gargoyles and so on. If you stick to the tripod you will be surprised at the amount of detail a 200mm lens will reveal in architectural close-ups. To photograph the famous carved Imp in Lincoln Cathedral, England, requires a lens of 500 to 1000mm!

Above: a modern detail in soft focus by *Alan Beastall.* **Top right:** interior from a high viewpoint, by *David Mark.* **Centre:** a traditional interior, 24mm lens, by *David Kilpatrick.* **Bottom:** looking upwards to a ceiling, with flash, by *Raymond Lea.*

Nothing rewards a photographer better than travel – it broadens the picture files as well as the mind. You may be torn between taking all the camera equipment you own and feeling weighed down, or missing some out and perhaps seeing a shot which needed one item you left behind. Most professional travel photographers agree that it is better to be mobile, and see more subjects, than to carry too much equipment and miss shots.

This makes the one-touch 35mm compact camera, with its pocketability and instant focus and exposure settings, an ideal travelling companion. You can take your SLR kit with wide-angle, standard, zoom and flash but also take a pocketable camera for the days when you want to enjoy the sun and fun. There is no *ideal film* for travel photography because light conditions can change anywhere in the world. Use the film you are most used to and get the best results from. An ISO 100/21° type is probably the best choice.

Take plenty of film unless you are travelling to a country where you know film is both fresh and cheap. In most countries, it is expensive and has been left for many months in hot kiosks. The airport X-ray machines will harm any films faster than ISO 400/27° and are not guaranteed to leave other films totally unmarked, whatever the officials may say. If you have just two or three films, take them out of the camera case and put them in your pocket to pass customs. If you have many, use a special Film Shield lead-foil travel pouch and put your films in the suitcase baggage which goes in the aircraft hold – this is normally given less X-ray dosage than hand baggage, and often receives none.

Do not risk local processing for important films, but by all means try it for anything you want to see at the time; you can get a 24-hour service almost anywhere in the world for Kodak C41 process colour print films. Never use local slide film processing or try the 'local' address on your process-paid mailer – it may simply take too long to come back.

Below: the high drama of travel is best captured on slide film, which can record subtle monochromatic scenes like this accurately. Colour prints tend to look very grey in comparison. Shot on Agfachrome film by *Clifford Mark*.

Travel outfits

The perfect travelling outfit is a wide-angle or wide-angle zoom lens of around 24–35mm, a standard lens with a fast aperture for night shots, and a tele zoom lens of around 70–210mm or 70–150mm for the sake of smaller size and lightness. With these lenses, you should ideally have not one but two SLR camera bodies. This enables you to keep shooting in the event of a breakdown, or use two bodies fitted with different lenses at interesting set-piece events which move quickly.

An *underwater* or beachproof camera like the Minolta Weathermatic, Fujica HD-S or Hanimex Amphibian is ideal for any seaside holiday. Apart from the ability to take your camera windsurfing or diving, you have no worries on the beach. An unprotected camera will be ruined by blown sand or salt spray and you will invalidate any warranty on a normal camera by exposing it to either. Special waterproof housings can be obtained for one-touch and SLR 35mm cameras, ranging from simple pouches to deep-sea diving kits.

Above: a 24–35mm zoom helped make this very colourful shot of fishing boats in Corfu, on Fujichrome 50 slide film.
Left: a 70–210mm zoom enabled a comfortable working distance in an Arab market for this portrait. Both photographs by *David Kilpatrick*.

Insure your camera outfit properly and check that your regular insurance covers you for the period you intend to spend abroad. Some insurance policies exclude certain countries, have limits which are far below the value of

91

your outfit, set excess figures on each individual piece of equipment rather than a whole kit, and so on.

Never wear your camera or case over your shoulder and slung behind you, especially in South and Central America and Asia. The value of the equipment is perfectly well-known in markets and expert thieves simply use a sharp knife to cut the straps. Wear the camera in front of you even if you feel like a typical tourist! Be careful when photographing locals in Asia and Africa, as there may be religious or superstitious objections to your intentions. It is better to use sign-language and point to the camera, then the planned subject. A exchange of petty cash may be involved but this is better than an exchange of abuse or fists. It is hard to find anywhere where the camera is not totally familiar today.

Exposure and light

If you live in a Northern temperate climate you may find it surprising that the camera does not always think you need sunglasses; the exposure it recommends seems much the same as on a sunny day at home, except when you get on the beach.

This is true. Trust the camera, and do not think that you have to reduce the exposure. In fact, there are some circumstances where the camera will indicate too little exposure and you may think it is behaving correctly. This happens when there are white walls and dusty streets, and most of the scene is very light in colour. The metering system assumes this is a normal scene, very brightly lit, and the result is therefore a greyish brown version of a white and gold original! Faced with a light sand beach, bleached village, limestone landscape, or snowy mountainside increase the exposure by one step or re-set your ISO film speed to half its normal value as long as you are shooting this kind of scene.

Do the same, even on dull days, with views of open sea. The sea will otherwise record as a very dark and unpleasantly grey colour. As a general rule, if you have not much experience with exposure it is better to use colour negative film for prints when travelling rather than to try colour slide film. Set the ISO speed rating permanently to half its normal value.

Heat

Colour film deteriorates with age, and the process is speeded up by heat. Never leave your film or camera in a place where is can get very hot. The glove compartments or shelves of cars are the worst places, followed by black coloured camera bags left in the sun. Colour film may produce degraded colours if left in the heat this way. You camera may be permanently damaged because the fine lubricating greases on the moving parts will melt and run off, leading to sticky focusing and wind-on actions and eventually to excessive wear and failure.

Subjects

When travelling, look for things which are different and interesting. Include local signs and names or streets, to remind you later of the circumstances. Take close-ups of details as well as scenes, and every time you take a picture with a friend in it, take another with the friend missed out. It is better to shoot your family's activities – water sports, riding horses, bargaining in the bazaar – and show what you *did*, then show *where* you went without the distraction of familiar faces in every scene.

Opposite top: a bright sky and snow in a Northern European scene produced minimal exposure for *Kevin Jelley* using an automatic SLR, capturing the winter feel of the location.

Opposite bottom: the Mediterranean sun produces strong, warm colours rather than bleached-out shades as sunset approaches. The limestone fortress of Les Baux was photographed by *David Kilpatrick* on 6 × 6cm film.

Below: it is better to put a friend in your shots as part of a real scene or composition, not just standing in the foreground. Here *Lorentz Gullachsen* saw the appeal of the agavi hedged track and asked his model to walk down it, shooting when the composition was right.

CHILDREN AND BABIES

Below: concentration enabled a candid indoor shot on fast VR1000 film for *Gerry Bater*.
Bottom: spontaneous shots are always the best – by *D. F. Whyte*.

The auto-exposure, auto-focus camera is ideal for photographing children and babies, whether your own family or not. Unless you are trying to make a formal portrait such as a seated mother and child or an older child, the subject will be hard to control and move quicker than you do.

Most autofocus cameras have lenses of around 35mm focal length, or moderately wide angle. One-touch compact 35mms rarely focus closer than 1 metre. These factors make it hard to get good shots of very small toddlers and babies. If you go close enough for a full face shot, the result is badly blurred, so you have to accept pictures which show everything from head to toe.

It's important not to aim the camera *down* at children, because this creates a gnome-like appearance with a big head and small body. Get down to their own level, on your knees, even lying down – or put the child on a chair, or swing, or a tree stump to bring the subject up to your level instead.

Getting down like this, or lifting the child, has a second effect. It makes the child less shy, and less dominated by this big adult with a camera who's getting annoyed about not being able to take the right picture!

Babies are *not* harmed by flash, regardless of their age. It would be unkind to fire a flash very close to a baby, but no damage would result. At a distance which would cause discomfort, your own camera's lens would be in more danger from small fingers. It can often be a good idea to fire a flash once, to attract attention, and then catch the interested anticipation. After the second or third shot interest wanes.

Some cameras have beeping sounds when used indoors. These signals can be interesting to young children. So can the flashing signals on the front of cameras with an electronic self-timing delay device. This works with toddlers, who can be told to watch the little light and see if it starts going faster. Just when it does, the shutter fires and you get the right expression.

For better pictures of children, a 35mm SLR fitted with a standard lens is by no means a bad choice. You can usually focus very close without difficulty and take telling close-ups of a sleeping baby, with a wide maximum aperture like f1.7 to allow pictures without flash in a well-lit room. Some hospitals will allow you to photograph newly-born babies as long as you do not use flash and it is not unusual to be able to photograph the birth itself.

For this, a lens like a 50mm f1.4 and a fast film of ISO 400 to 1600 speed are recommended.

A slightly longer focus lens, such as the 'portrait' short telephoto 85mm to 100mm, enables candid pictures of older children who do not realise they are the sole subject of the picture. If you keep a couple of metres away, they will often get on with playing and ignore the camera. An autofocus SLR helps because children move too fast for reliable focusing with lenses longer than 50mm. Zoom lenses, of around 70–210mm, are a bit frightening for very small children and definitely put a barrier up between you and them.

Perhaps the ideal compromise is the 35–85mm zoom, avoiding those makes which only focus to 1m or have restricted maximum apertures like f4.5. A 35–85mm f2.8 with focusing down to 75cm would be ideal for family shots. It can catch anything from a small group running around outdoors to a quietly posed facial portrait of a teenager.

Bounce flash is more successful with shots of toddlers and babies than it is with adults. The subject is probably two metres away from the ceiling instead of less than 1 metre, and you are probably lower down as well, so the bounce illumination travels further and is much more diffused. You don't get the same heavy eye-shadow and

chin-shadow effects. Small children often roll around or lie on their backs, and as long as the background is suitable you can get extremely well-lit results with simple bounce flash. You must always use a fast film, because quick focusing at apertures like f4 (required with bounce flash for slower films) may lead to unsharp results.

Top left: a simple outdoor portrait can be taken on any camera, but backlighting improves it. By *A. Johnson.*
Top right: dramatic colours and action make a very unusual shot for *Peter Karry* with a wide-angle lens.
Above: a medium telephoto and careful timing help at events and on holiday. *David Kilpatrick* used a shutter speed of 1/1000 to freeze the action.

Professional photographers use a little camera technique and a good deal of 'man management' to assure good wedding and group photographs. A little confidence combined with basic knowledge of their methods can help improve your own shots.

The first rule for group photography is to have an odd number of people in the group if you can. Three people in a shot looks better than four; five looks better than six. If you have an even number, use two rows – arrange four people as a line of three plus one positioned to the front and lower down. The second rule is to arrange the group into a curved line, not a straight one, so that the people at the edges of the picture are just the same distance from the camera as the ones in the middle. This is important when using wide-angle lenses indoors, or the central person could be much nearer the lens and would appear bigger in the picture. Finally, in large groups don't be afraid to ask a few people to squat, sit or kneel to form a front row lower down and compose the shot better both in terms of odd/even number balance and filling the 35mm frame shape.

The camera can only focus on a single point, so in a perfect group shot, everyone is at about the same distance or within a foot or so. The front row touches the back row. To avoid ugly gaps, you ask everyone to stand close together. You can compress the length of the line even more if you ask them to stand sideways to the camera (those at the edges of the shot face inwards, not outwards) and just turn their heads face-on to the lens.

With flash, it is particularly important to follow the rule of keeping the group within a foot or so of total depth. Never photograph a three-tier group with a one-touch camera or an SLR fitted with a wide-angle lens; get back, and use a lens of 50–85mm. Then the effect of distance on the flash intensity (the Inverse Square Law) will be minimized, and you will not end up with white front-row faces and deep red back-row faces. Remember that some flashguns are positioned to one side of the camera lens, not directly above it. Adjust the group so that shadow of each member does not fall on the face of a person behind.

At weddings, the professional photographer will not photograph a white-wedding bride in direct sunshine. Instead, he will turn the bride's back to the sun and use backlight with adjusted exposure, or

Right: a group calls for careful arrangement even if fairly informal. The overall depth should not be so great that it exceeds the depth of field, and some members may have to kneel or sit to make a large group fit the available space. If every person in the group can see the camera clearly, then their faces should be visible in the final picture.

perhaps a little fill-in flash. This can have the secondary effect of preventing guests equipped with simple cameras from taking good shots, but no professional has this as a principal motive. The reason is to stop glare and excessive contrast from a fully lit white dress next to a dark suit.

For flash pictures of the bride and groom, the groom takes the position nearest to the camera even if the bride is more important. This also applies when photographing a cake cutting – the bride, and the cake, are both slightly further away than the groom. This compensates for the problems of flash illumination.

If the bride is closer to the camera, her white dress will be totally burned-out in the print. By putting the dark-suited groom where he gets more light than the white bride and cake, the photographer evens out the lighting and contrast.

In church, many ministers dislike flash exposures but will allow quiet photography on a tripod by natural light. There are many pauses in the service where everyone is still, and an exposure of about 1 second will be sharp. Make sure you do not include a large area of stained glass window in your viewfinder, or this may be the only properly exposed thing you see in the final print. Base the exposure on the floor area of the church.

Close-ups are rarely taken by wedding guests, and sometimes missed out by the official photographer. With a one-touch autofocus compact camera, you can catch appealing incidents with children and throw yourself into the general affray if confetti is thrown – just aim at the bride, in the middle of the falling confetti, and shoot freely. You will probably end up with the most spontaneous, memorable shot at the wedding. To photograph a bride and groom inside a wedding car, you need a lens of 28 or 24mm focal length. Ask the couple to squeeze together at the far end of the seat – it looks natural in the final print – and use flash.

There are other formal occasions where the camera can be needed. To photograph an after-dinner speaker or a lecturer, use flash and a lens of around 85–135mm on a 35mm SLR. Do not use a zoom lens of around

200mm, because in most rooms the smoke in the air starts to cast a mist over the image at distances over three or four metres.

A dinner table group, round a circular table seating eight, can be photographed with a one-touch camera or an SLR with a 35mm or 28mm lens. Tables are normally too close together to allow you to use a 50mm. Ask three people from one side of the table to get up and stand behind the other five, who should shuffle a little closer together. With flash, the white tablecloth can burn out in the foreground, so avoid including too much of it.

For graduations and formal portraits of graduates in gowns, give slightly more exposure than the camera or flash indicates. This ensures a neutral black gown rather than risking a brownish or purplish result.

Above: when taking a portrait, or a shot lit with flash, of a bride and groom which involves both dark and light clothing try to have the darker clothing nearer to the camera and the lighter outfit further away. This gives an evenly-lit result in the final print. The same applies to faces; people with dark or ruddy-complexioned faces should be nearer to the camera and flash unit than those with light skin.

SPECIAL EFFECTS

Complicated photo effects are so common in television, video and advertising that the results from your camera may be a little 'tame'. It is possible to create some simple effects with any camera and attachments are sold to produce these to order.

Multiple exposure is only possible with some models of SLR, and hardly ever with compact 35mms. The film has to stay still, while the shutter is re-cocked. In some cases a special button is provided to allow double or repeated exposures, in others you have to go through a sequence of pressing the film rewind button, holding the film rewind lever to prevent movement, and winding on with the normal advance lever. If this method is workable the makers' instructions normally describe how to do it.

Successful multi-exposure needs planning. The first picture has to have a dark area, where the light coloured detail of the second shot can appear. Ideally, the second picture should not affect existing detail in the first.

Remember that *light* always takes precedence. You can not double expose a dark object seen on a white background on top of a light coloured scene. If you took a beach picture, then photographed a ball on a white table on the same frame, you would not get a giant ball on a beach. The result would be a very light picture with a ghost image of the ball, and degraded colours.

If you shot a city street at dusk, with a deep blue sky overhead, and then double-exposed a close-up of a light bulb hanging on a wire in a dark-painted room so that the bulb fell into the sky area, the result would be a total success; light second exposure superimposed on a dark area of the first shot.

Multiple flash exposure can be fun, outdoors where there is no background to record. Ask someone to move around while you take several flash pictures on the same frame. You will have a whole group of cloned people in the shot! Sometimes, casual double

Below: using a camera with a special control to allow multiple exposures, *Martin Lillicrap* took two shots in succession on the same frame of film at the British Royal Silver Jubilee celebrations to sum up the event.

or multi-exposure makes a visually intriguing shot even when the rules are broken. Experiment never harmed any photographer.

Long time exposure is only possible in dim lighting with a slow film, and has special applications in action and night time photography. In daylight, a special filter can be bought which screws to the front of the lens and reduces the light by 4, 8, 16 or even up to 100,000 times. With the camera on a tripod, you can photograph a busy city scene using an exposure of several minutes or even hours. Only those parts of the scene which stay perfectly still, like a parked car, are recorded. Pedestrians and vehicles just disappear – they pass through the scene so quickly, in terms of the exposure time, that they are not recorded.

The same method can be used to turn violently moving parts of a picture into a ghostly blur or mist. Try this technique with the sea at sunset, when long exposures are easy.

Any time longer than 20 seconds will turn the waves into a kind of fog. This technique works well with waterfalls, streams, waving windblown grass or a jaccuzzi. It does not work well with trees as the sky behind them tends to wipe out the detail of branches.

Left: a special filter giving a streaked image, combined with a purple colour polarizer, turned a wood into an abstract for *Chris Mole.*

Below: a long time exposure by the lights of a night-time colliery recorded the smoke as a flowing mist in this shot by *Alan Beastall.*

Above: a dark blue graduated filter used to cover the sky area controlled contrast and added colour to this shot by *Chris Mole,* taken using a wide-angle lens.

Right: *John Cummings* recorded this 'meteor shower' using point sources of light and a diffraction grating to split white light into rainbow colours with directional streaking.

Prismatic optics are screwed on the front of the camera lens, like filters, and split the picture into a set of overlapping part-images. The central one is usually sharp, surrounded by satellite versions which may be equally sharp, softened, or perhaps coloured. Other prisms have a sharp image at one end of the picture, with a string of closely spaced repeating images giving an effect of speed or movement trailing behind.

Filter effects range from a simple soft-focus which takes the 'bite' out of portrait shots and improves skin tones, to holographically produced patterns which turn any light source in the picture into a rainbow burst of coloured lines. Some filters give the image a sharp centre, and blurred edges. Others impart a linear streaking to half of the shot for a motion effect. One useful type shades the sky down to a darker colour, or adds false colour, with a smooth transition in the middle of the picture so that the change is not visible; these are called graduated filters, and the most useful

one is light blue, for improving plain white skies.

Mattes are like filters, and fit in front of the lens, but are used in conjunction with double or multiple exposure. The

two most popular types are half-and-half and central spot. One matte mask is used to cover half the picture for the first exposure; a precisely matched other half is then put in its place, so that the other half of the shot can be exposed. This way, the same person can appear twice in an otherwise normal scene. The central spot matte allows you to photograph a bouquet of flowers to form a 'frame', then a portrait of a girl to go in the centre. Unless the matte is very well made

and the camera and lens totally suited to it, the join may be visible as a slightly dark or light blurred area.
Moonlight can be imitated when using colour slides (but not prints, as these will be corrected during printing). You fit a medium blue filter of the type used to correct daylight colour film when shooting in tungsten room lighting, but use this in normal daylight, and underexpose the picture by about one stop. This works best with suitable subjects like seascapes.

Left: a genuine moonlight shot on daylight colour slide film, taken in the Lake District by *David Gordon* using a very long exposure. A deep blue filter imitates this effect in daytime.

Below left: a graduated tobacco-colour filter enhances a sunset – by *Percy Willoughby*.

Below: soft focus diffuses this outdoor fashion shot by *John Xavier*, who made his own filter from perspex, sandpapered until the effect was judged to be right.

NIGHT PHOTOGRAPHY

Most 35mm cameras with built-in exposure systems will give you an accurate meter reading from a brightly-lit street at night, but they can not operate in moonlight or indoors by firelight and similar very low illumination. A separate hand-held exposure meter, often recommended for low light work, must be extremely good and probably expensive to do much better.

At night, the best advice is to take several shots and make some informed guesses. Film manufacturers may include a useful guide to suggested exposures with fast films – have a look at the leaflet which comes with your film. *Dusk* is the best time to take night pictures of streets and cities, because there is still enough light in the sky to record as a deep blue glow. The same twilight helps relieve the shadows from street lamps, and generally improves the colour and contrast of the scene. At dusk, your camera should still work reliably.

City lights recorded on their own, with no need to show the general scene or buildings, do not need a very long exposure. Move close to a sign, and see what the camera says. You will probably be able to use a setting of around 1/30th at f4 on ISO 100 film, so even fairly restricted lenses like a 70–210mm zoom can be used with adequate support. Try operating the zooming action during an exposure of around 1 second when shooting city lights – it can create an interesting explosion of colours.

Street scenes without illuminated signs normally need much longer exposure, around 1/4 of second at f4 with ISO 100 film, as long as there are brightly lit shop windows throwing pools of light on the passers-by. Orange sodium street lamps are not suitable for photography, and the results tend to be very dark. Allow extra exposure where the main lighting is from sodium or any other strongly-coloured light. Shop windows themselves can be photographed hand-held, but remember that the lighting in them will record yellowish-orange on slide film.

Below: night shots can be taken hand-held with care, as this view of Dundee and the Tay Bridge in Scotland shows. It was taken at full aperture on a 50mm f1.4 lens by *D. Worthington* at about 1/30th of a second on daylight slide film.

TV screens and computer displays in windows, or at home, should be photographed using a shutter speed of 1/15th of a second or longer to avoid lines appearing on the image. The normal exposure for a colour video screen at regular brightness is 1/15th at f2 with ISO 100 film, but for static displays like computer graphics a setting of 1 second at f8 will produce better results. Do not rely on automatic exposure metering. Cine screens can not be photographed conventionally.

Theatre and concert lighting is bright enough for action pictures if you have the right lens and film. An ISO 1000 speed film is ideal, and will allow shutter speeds of around 1/250–1/500 at an aperture of between f4 and f8 with most theatrical spotlights and stage acts. The best type of lens to choose is a fast telephoto – an 85mm f2, 135mm f2.8,

200mm f2.8 or similar. You may find restrictions placed on photography at major events, but circuses, small theatres and open-air concerts may allow it. There is no point in using flash under any circumstances unless you are on stage yourself! The distance is just too great for any effect.

Bonfires, fireworks, festive lights and similar subjects need much the same approach, but large fires can often just be photographed by an auto exposure hand held. Fireworks need an exposure of around f8 on ISO 100 film, if you keep the shutter open for around 5–10 seconds.

Light trails are a popular outdoor subject, which you can produce anywhere there is a major traffic interchange. It's better to aim at departing traffic, catching the tail lights, and to have any oncoming traffic strictly over to one side and occupying little of the picture. Pick a

Above left: fast ISO 1600 colour negative film allowed an exposure of 1/250 at f5.6 with a 70–210mm zoom lens for *Richard Bradbury* at the final concert by group Status Quo.

Above right: *Simon Kemp* fitted a multi-image prism over his lens to shoot this hand-held exposure of fireworks.

Over page: a range of night-time images – **top,** light streaks by *Michael Lear,* below, diffraction filtered lights by *Dr Keith Hewitt;* **bottom,** an eastern market by *J. M. Currie* and Lake Geneva by *Peter Cooke.*

viewpoint like a footbridge, so that you can look down the road, and set the camera on a tripod. Use an aperture like f8, and try exposures of 10 seconds to one minute. Then try other apertures, like f11 and f16, in the same way. Avoid opening the shutter during the time that a car is passing, or a trail will start suddenly in mid-picture. Indicator lights appear as broken lines and brake lights as a thickening and brightening of an existing line for a short period.

Water is an ally, not an enemy, whenever you are shooting lights or scenes which contain many lights. Harbours, wet streets, ponds or fountains can all reflect the lights so that the total number appears to be doubled in your picture, and the otherwise empty foreground is full of life. Reflections in glass can be made to do the same thing but lack the variety or distortion and spread available when lights are reflected off water. Long exposures of lights over moving water will produce a soft effect just as they do in daylight.

Finally, remember that some night-time subjects are highly photogenic. Steam or smoke caught in the light looks excellent, and a heavy fog or mist can transform an untidy street scene. So can snow, creating night time shots which are almost as easy to compose and shoot as daylight ones. Railway stations, subways, factories, bus stations, airports, floodlit buildings, church interiors by candlelight, and many other subjects can be found at night.

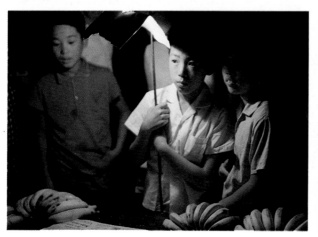

FLOWERS AND PLANTS

Garden flowers and plants may find a special place in your photographic album because they are temporary and change from season to season. A particularly spectacular display may last only a few days. In public gardens or on holiday you may see plants which you would like to grow, but can not identify. Photography helps here by providing a permanent record which can be much more accurate than a drawing or a description.

Plants are not static subjects. Unless the air is very still, they move as much in proportion to their size as an active child! This movement does not matter much for a general view of a flower-border, but it can be enough to prevent easy close-ups of a single bloom.

The best equipment for flower and plant photography is a 35mm SLR fitted with a zoom and a screw-in close-up lens. These lenses are available in different strengths – 1 dioptre sets the lens focus to 1 metre or less, +2 dioptre to 50cm or less, +3 dioptres to 33cm or less. The close-up lens decides the *furthest* working distance, and you can no longer focus on infinity.

You can buy more powerful close-up lenses such as +4 (25cm) or even +10 (10cm) but it you intend to go as close as this, a proper macro lens with continuous focusing down to life size or half life-size is much better. A 90 or 100mm macro lens is preferable to a 50mm, because you are then able to take the same size subject from twice as far away.

The method using close-up lenses on ordinary zooms is suggested because you can stand even further away than normal, and by adjusting the zoom setting of a typical lens like a 70–210mm, you can frame up different sizes of plant. All the fully automatic functions of your camera are retained

and there is no need for exposure corrections when using flash. Special macro lenses often need increased exposure as you focus closer. The zoom lens plus close-up attachment method ensures the highest possible shutter speed, which helps cut out unsharpness caused by slight vibration or sudden movement of the plant in the wind. In poor lighting, switch to flash rather than a tripod for exactly the same reason. The only time you can use a tripod is inside a glasshouse or with very solid subjects like cacti.

Below: a cactus flower is normally static enough for a time exposure with a tripod, and a small aperture for depth of field. By *John Rawlings*. The small picture by *Alan Welsh* shows the opposite approach, using a wider aperture and differential focus for a small part of a more fragile flower.

Depth of field is critical in flower and plant photography. You must have sufficient sharpness in depth to render all parts of the main subject clearly, but the background should be thrown out of focus to avoid any possible confusion. A depth-of-field preview on your SLR is almost essential, and some of the lower-cost models do not have this facility. There are two ways of overcoming the problem of keeping the subject within the zone of best sharpness, and losing the background.

The simplest method, usable with any lens or camera, is to align your field of view with the subject as 'flat' as possible to the camera. If you are photographing a dahlia bloom, take the shot from above so that the flower makes a circle of flat petals. Do not photograph it from sideways on, although this may show the stem and leaves better. The 'flat on' shot will be sharp from edge to edge; the 'side on' shot would probably have some badly out-of-focus petals. The second method is to use flash positioned off the camera, on an extension cable, so that only the subject is illuminated and the background is dead black shadow.

The criticism of flash used this way is that the environment is not shown, and some delicate flowers need softer lighting. You can probably devise other solutions as well, such as carefully lifting the specimen and 'replanting' it in front of a neutral background in better lighting, or placing a small background card behind it. A green or blue card, thrown slightly out of focus, can look like foliage or the sky. The choice of colour is important.

A *water spray* is often used by plant photographers to give the specimens a fresh look, but you should never spray a flower when the sun is bright; the droplets of water act as small lenses and may scar the plant by burning it. Vegetables and cut flowers look good presented in a traditional garden trug or wicker basket, and fruit can be taken indoors or into a studio. Make sure that you use the exposure over-ride to give +1 stop of extra exposure when photographing fruit or foliage with a light sky as a background. Against a deep blue sky, normal exposure is correct.

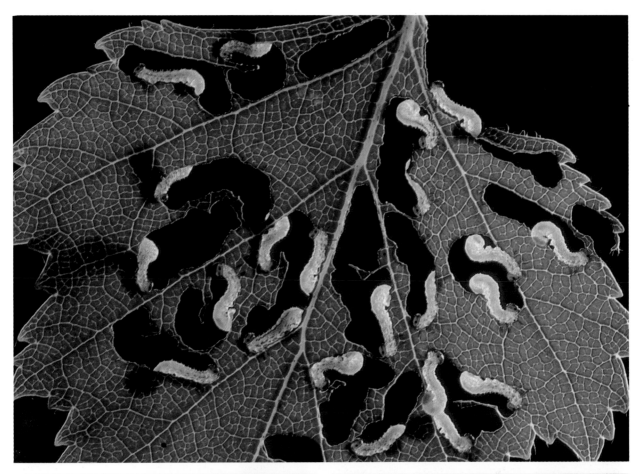

A *polarizing filter* works wonders with the colours of flowers and foliage in sunshine, by cutting out the sheen or gloss of white reflected light on the waxy surface of the plant. The best time to use a polarizer is when the sun is midway in the sky, not at noon or very early or late, on general scenes rather than close-ups. The deeper blue sky and improved greens, most noticeable on conifers and darker coloured plants, will change the result totally. Trees or shrubs which

originally looked 'dark' against a bright sky may seem 'bright' against a rich blue. For close-ups, the polarizer is less successful. This filter requires from two to four times the normal exposure, and any exposure increases are undesirable in close-up work. The surface sheen which it eliminates helps give three-dimensional shape and texture to small subjects, and is best left intact. With a polarizer, close-ups of plants and flowers may have purer colours but can look lifeless.

Opposite top: a flower kept parallel to the camera for sharpness, by *David Kilpatrick*. **Below:** flash and a black backdrop, by *Martin Lillicrap* in the studio.

Top: sawfly larvae on a leaf, lit with flash by *Duncan McEwan*. **Above:** the effect of a shot without (left) and with (right) a polarizing filter – *David Kilpatrick*.

Film choice is straightforward for garden photography – use a colour slide film of medium speed if you possibly can. This is the only way to ensure accurate colours, and even then some shades of pink and blue blooms will show false colours. Colour negative film records everything just as well, but colour casts introduced during printing such specific subjects will probably spoil the shot. This applies more to the close-ups than distant views.

Avoid high speed films, although they are easier to use. The greens and pure colours are not as good as those on films of ISO 200 speed or lower. There is a special infra-red sensitive film available, more for the advanced worker, in both colour and black and white. This film gives false colours or changed tones, and can differentiate between healthy and diseases or dried-up foliage.

For all plant photography, a camera with off-the-film flash exposure control is a great advantage. Specialized accessories like shadow-free ringflash and extension bellows to allow high magnifications are only necessary if you plan to tackle very small specimens indeed.

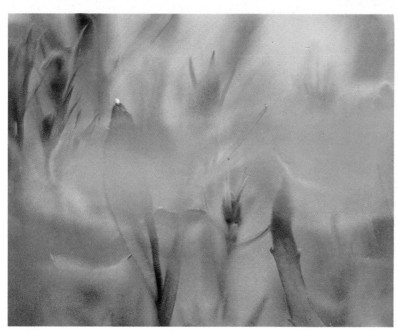

Top: slow, fine grain Kodachrome 25 film gave the brightest colours and highest sharpness to these fungi photographed by *Duncan McEwan*. **Above left:** a radically different approach to flower photography, with a diffused soft colour abstract from *Kim Mullineux*. **Above right:** *Bernard Child* used a wide-angle lens and a ground level viewpoint to keep the sun behind these sugar cane plants and set them in backlit relief against a blue sky.

COLOUR STUDIES

Colour slide film is able to reproduce very subtle and very saturated colours with equal accuracy, and because there is no printing process, whatever exposure you give in the camera is translated to a light, normal or dark result. Keep your eyes open and you will find that there are hundreds of colourful close-ups and studies to be taken, forming abstract designs or patterns, where the colour is the main subject.

It is possible to shoot this kind of picture on colour negative film, for prints, but whenever the frame is filled with one colour the printer will tend to 'correct' this imbalance. As a result, a shot of a badge on a yellow taxi cab will have extra blue put into the picture and you end up with a slightly cold greenish-yellow. Colour negative film only works well if all the colours in the picture are balanced. A shot of a bunch of red, green, yellow and blue balloons would be printed perfectly – so would a single red balloon against a blue sky. A blue balloon against a blue sky would probably be printed as an overall steel-grey result.

The secret to a 'normal' colour balance in colour negative shots is to pick *complementary* or opposite colours, and for this you need some knowledge of colour theory. Generally speaking, a warm colour (red, magenta, yellow, orange, brown) in equal proportion to a cool colour (blue, violet, green, cyan, purple) within a picture will produce a good balance.

Left: *Ruth Bowtell* found paints on a palette in a simple colour combination, and eliminated all unwanted detail by closing right in.

Below: subtle and glowing colours like these Seychelles fish photographed by *Mike Travers* reproduce better on slide film than negative. He used Kodachrome 64.

Above left: three primary colours stand out against neutral black in this ultra-wide-angle studio composition by *Richard Bradbury*.

Above right: four primary colours, accentuated by through-lighting, found in a golf umbrella close-up by *David Copling*.

Right: muted monochromatic colours, with a single red hue against an almost black and white frame, seen by *Peter Williams*.

Here are the actual opposite colours which will 'integrate' to grey if matched against each other:

Yellow	Blue
Magenta	Green
Cyan (blue-green)	Red

In colour slide pictures, the only constraints are aesthetic. Contrasts of colours do not always look good, and often a set of closely related hues or tints in a single colour will make a better picture. Slide films have their own colour balance, and some are higher in contrast than others, but once you have chosen the film you like personally it should still be able to distinguish changes in shade which your own eyes find hard to spot.

Paintwork provides many detailed and colourful close-up studies. All you need for this is a sunny day and a camera with a standard 50mm lens. Old doors, with peeling layers of paint and interesting knockers or numberplates, are conveniently flat subjects which can be photographed at

wide apertures and fast shutter speeds for ultimate sharpness.

Nature is not always green and in the autumn, fallen leaves can provide a palette of related warm colours. Rocks, sand, tree bark, and many other everyday finds make good colour studies.

Architectural detail on modern buildings provides more room for colour and for abstract compositions than on older buildings, which tend to use natural materials in natural colours. Vehicles, fairgrounds, seaside structures, kiosks and shanty-town shacks can have brilliant colours or weatherworn and faded ones. Markets and street traders with wares laid out provide another source of random composition which you, by selecting an area with viewfinder, can turn into photo art.

The common factor in all colour studies of this type is that you are selecting a frame and concentrating on it. A particular street detail or a corner of an Eastern market stall might not catch the eye of the average passer-by, but once you have studied it through

the camera and isolated the picture you want it could well sum up the atmosphere of a place far better than a general scene. You hardly ever need wide-angle or telephoto lenses for this type of work, unless your subject is hard to get at, and using flash seems

Top: deliberate underexposure to boost colour saturation, by *Duncan McEwan*. **Above:** man-made colours in architectural detail, by *David Kilpatrick*.

Opposite: *Martin Lillicrap* used an ordinary hair-comb and coloured lights, with a water spray, for this superb 35mm studio shot.

Right: the selective angle of view of a 500mm mirror lens enabled *David Kilpatrick* to close in on the backs of donkies for sale in a North African market and produce a composition in colour and texture.

Below: a contrasting approach in a travel shot by *Alan Welsh* taken with a wide-angle lens and featuring several bright, contrasting colours.

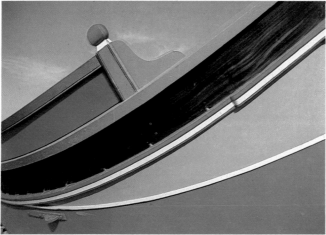

to kill the effects of natural lighting which are essential to the shot.

Colour studies like this are increasingly popular in photo magazines, as wall posters, in contests and as home decoration where a related set of colours or subjects can be made into a set of framed enlargements. There is still no word to describe this kind of photography! It isn't still life, pictorial, landscape or close-up as such. Colour is the most important single aspect. What is most exciting is that any camera owner can have a go at this type of shot.

BLACK AND WHITE PHOTOGRAPHY

Above: two examples of situations which make good black and white shots, both taken by *Raymond Lea*. Colour would not add much to either scene.

Monochrome photography does not have to be black and white, because many things can be done with a black and white shot when you process it at home. It can be turned into a brown (sepia) print, converted to an abstract colour image using dyes and toners, or printed on to aluminium plaques.

Most photographers who try black and white find that it is rewarding and exciting enough just to make their own prints, without any of this creative after-treatment. Pictures which do not seem to work in colour sometimes succeed in black and white. The simplification of the image into a series of tones between white and black, without the distraction of colour, improves compositional impact. It also removes the picture one step from reality, and makes it more of a deliberate work of art or craft.

Black and white films are available in exactly the same speed ranges as colour films, and are used in precisely the same way for ordinary pictures. Specialist services will process them for you but this is now more expensive than colour developing and printing.

Home processing is not only cheaper, but most of the fun in black and white. You do not require a darkroom for film processing (see the section on the Home Darkroom, pages 141–153) but for printing, you have to be able to black a room out.

Once you have shot and processed a black and white film, the print can be adjusted over a wide range of possible final effects. You can control brightness and contrast, much as you can on a television set, by selecting different 'grades' of printing paper and giving different degrees of exposure. It is thus possible to turn the same shot into a softly-toned, bright scene or a powerful dark silhouette. This is not the case with colour printing, where the only adjustments you can make are in the density of the image (over a limited range) and the colour balance.

Some control is also possible in the camera, by varying the exposure, but it is best to stick to the recommended settings. If you do make a mistake and under or over expose a negative, the same degree of control which allows creative printing also enables *corrective* printing.

High contrast scenes photograph well in black and white, and large areas of dark shadow can be printed as a rich pure black. Subjects like a directly against-the-light silhouette, which would not be acceptable for a colour print, can be taken in black and white.

Filters have a different role in monochrome. For colour shots, the effect of a filter can be seen through the viewfinder after you fit the filter to the lens. In monochrome, there are three important filters – yellow, orange and red. These do not colour the picture, but alter the way the film records some tones.

A yellow filter corrects the natural oversensitivity of the film to blue light, which otherwise makes white clouds in a pale blue sky come out as a plain white sky with no clouds. The yellow filter brings out the sky and the clouds and makes the scene look normal. The orange filter, which is stronger, turns the blue sky a darker grey but leaves the clouds brilliant white. It also lightens skin tones and all orange, red or yellow subjects in the shot. The effect can be fairly dramatic.

The red filter is so strong that the sky may record as almost black, and even faint cirrus clouds are dramatically recorded. Red objects are shown as white or light grey, and foliage is also rendered as much lighter because the green colour of trees and grass actually hides a large red-orange content.

There are other colour filters which can be used in black and white, including a light green which darkens white skin tones and the sky at the same time, avoiding some of the problems with yellow filters, and a blue filter which gives good facial detail for portraits in artificial lighting. All these filters require an exposure increase, which is marked on the rim – 2× (1 stop extra) for yellow, 4× for orange (2 stops), 8× for red (3 stops). Some types of film, like Kodak Technical Pan and Ilford XP-1, do not require as much increase. The exposure systems of SLR cameras should take these factors into account automatically, in theory, but in practice the sensor cells are thrown off balance by the strong colours of the light.

It is better to take a meter reading

without the filter, and adjust the exposure when the filter is fitted. With black and white in general, medium speed films of around ISO 125 are the most consistently reliable and simple to use. There are special fine-grained films to give more detail, which have no equivalent in colour negative materials, and may be anything from ISO 25 to ISO 50. These films are difficult to use, require special development for the best results, and should be left until you are experienced with ordinary films. Fast

Above: a scene photographed in black and white (top) with no filter, and then (below) with a yellow filter to bring out the clouds against a blue sky. FP4 film, 24mm lens – *David Kilpatrick.*

ISO 400 films are fairly straightforward to use but processing needs to be a little more careful, and the prints may appear to show film grain to a greater degree than you are used to from colour films of the same speed.

Black and white photography is a craft best learned from someone who can demonstrate it, and joining a local photo evening class or attending a course is worthwhile.

Left: monochrome in gothic mood, by *Michael Maguire*. **Below:** the graphic potential of patterns and film grain, by *Raymond Lea*.

PHOTOGRAPHY AT WORK

Subject interest is the key to a successful photograph, and pictures taken at your workplace showing your colleagues in action will probably be popular with everybody – including your friends and family who like to see how you spend your 'other life'!

First of all, make sure that you are allowed to take pictures. Although your employer may not have preconceived objections, he could see it as a disruption to routine or even a danger. Many workers discard safety equipment and ignore regulations even after their company has provided all the right things, just because they find it easier to work without the hard hats, gloves, safety shoes and machinery guards required. If you took pictures showing this happening, you might get the firm and your workmates into trouble. Professional photographers often carry safety helmets and similar equipment in the back of their car when tackling industrial shots, not to wear but to lend to their subjects. If you can get proper clearance to take pictures, with the area tidied up and the people involved correctly dressed, your firm may even find them useful.

Lighting conditions are unpredictable in factories. Fluorescent lighting in office areas produces a strong green cast on colour films. To eliminate this, fit an FL-D type filter on slide films or allow one stop extra exposure with colour negative films. Sodium lighting produces orange results, even when it is not of the deep orange type but more 'normal' to the eye. An A-D correction may partly correct this. Tungsten lighting, from floodlights or luminaires with conventional bulbs, can be fully corrected using an 80C strong A-D type filter or one stop extra exposure for colour negatives. Finally, discharge lamps or mercury vapour lamps give a very cold purple cast which is not easily killed.

One of the most exciting things about factory lighting is that many of these light sources are often MIXED in a single shot, so that no correction should be used – instead, you can let the available daylight add to the exposure, and see extra colour put in by the contrast between sodium, mercury vapour, tungsten and fluorescent localized lighting.

Flash on the camera tends to spoil industrial pictures, unless there is plenty of interesting detail in the background. As ordinary flash shutter speeds do not let this detail record, the answer is to use a tripod and combine your flash exposure with a time exposure. Use colour negative film for your first experiments with this technique, as it has more latitude to exposure errors. Assuming the flash needs f8 for a subject at 2 metres

Below: a simple 35mm compact camera was used for both these shots of emergency work in a glassworks, by *Sheldon Davies*, on a one-touch 35mm auto exposure camera and slide film.

distance, take a reading for the whole scene without flash at the same aperture of f8. It may say the shutter needs to be open for 1/2 second. For the actual exposure, use the flash normally and use 1/2 second, but change the lens aperture f8 to between f8 and f11 – close it down by half a stop. This compensates for the fact that you are working out exposures for flash ALONE and time exposure ALONE, but using both TOGETHER.

Welding, grinding, pouring molten metals, opening furnaces and similar scenes have spectacular photographic possibilities because of the vividly coloured and dramatic lighting effects they produce.

For moderately bright subjects, in good general light, just take a normal exposure using a tripod. This would apply to removing a crucible from a benchtop furnace in a well-lit laboratory. Never use flash, because the effect will kill the red glow from the subject.

For glowing subjects in a darker situation, you may have to use flash to bring out some background detail. As long as you do not try to expose the scene fully with flash, but set your lens to a couple of stops less exposure than the flash requires, the result will be correct. If the flash is set for f8, then make your time exposure at f16.

Sometimes it is difficult to judge how much exposure to give a self-illuminated subject as you can not take a meter reading directly. This applies to computer screen displays as much as to hot metal. The solution is to use a portable floodlight or even a table lamp. Bring the lamp gradually closer to the subject, until the general brightness of the area all round it seems to be balanced with the subject itself. Then take a meter reading from this overall area.

After turning off your floodlight, use this exposure to shoot the subject alone. The principle is the same as the old 'grease spot photometer' light meters used in the early years of this century – light from a small bulb run from a battery was 'balanced' with existing light until a patch seen through an eyepiece disappeared. You are simply balancing the brightness of one source with another, and using

your ability to read the exposure for one to set the exposure for the other.

Very bright activities, like welding, usually act as a light source themselves. It is often enough just to aim the camera and shoot, but you will get better results from welding and grinding shots if the shutter stays open for around half a second. This allows traces of light to record as streaks on the film. To get this, close the lens down to f16, set auto on your camera, use a tripod, and shoot. Vary the exposure by using an over-ride control if available or changing the filmspeed setting (for ISO 100 film, try exposures at 25, 50, 200 and 400 settings as well as 100).

A *starburst* or cross-screen filter adds a great deal to pictures of welding, which often contain just a single bright point of light. The filter forms a brilliant star or cross of lines of light centred on this spot, and gives the same impression in the photograph that we seem to see by eye.

Some types of work offer unique photo opportunities. Any job which involves travelling turns 'pictures at work' into general scenes of towns, landscapes and so on which people who are office-bound have no chance to get. On building sites, you can climb to elevations well above the townscape and shoot 'aerial' views or unusual perspectives from cranes. For conditions where a camera might be damaged, try using a Ewa-Marine or similar flexible underwater housing, which holds an ordinary SLR or one-touch camera and allows relatively unhindered operation. You have to remove the camera from its case to reload film. There are several special cameras, like the Nikonos and Fujica HD models, which are intended to resist rain or spray and will also put up with fairly rough overall treatment.

News pictures crop up at work when accidents happen, particularly if you are a fireman or a rescue worker. It does seem wrong for anyone involved in emergency services to carry a camera for personal reasons, if only because the thought of a good picture might distract from the urgent work in hand. In fact, many people in these jobs do use cameras because the records of damage or disaster help in educating other people. Selling a picture to a newspaper is a different matter. You are free to photograph most scenes or situations if you are in a public place and do not invade anyone's privacy or use the picture for advertising. On private property, particularly corporate-owned factories or offices, you are not free to do this and might end up in court as a result.

There is a big demand for good pictures of people working, from newspapers, magazines and picture agencies as well as the firms themselves who may have brochures, exhibitions or company newspapers. Standards are high but there is no reason why your interest could not earn you appreciation and cash (or both) if you make the grade.

Some types of work lend themselves to particular pictures and effects. Welding and grinding, and pouring hot metal are obvious ones. Here is a slightly less common one – fabricating highly polished sheet stainless steel into a two foot diameter chimney. A wide-angle lens and a carefully positioned 'quality control man' help make the shot. Courtesy AI Sheet Metal Ltd; photograph by *David Kilpatrick*.

SUNSETS

No photographer can fail to be drawn to a spectacular sunset. It's probably the most popular scenic subject ever. Most sunsets are mediocre and fail because the scale of sun itself is too small, the colours are diluted, and the picture is simply not interesting.

West coast or shore locations make the best places to find sunsets. It does not matter much whether the water is a river, lake or ocean; even a garden pond can improve a sunset by reflecting the sky. This doubles the 'size' of the scene straight away. A wet street, wet sand or snow can have the same advantage.

For sunsets without any special equipment, look for dramatic clouds and some contrast in the colour. The sky should contain some blue, perhaps, with each cloud edged with red. Stormy days, clear evenings after rain, and bright windy days with very high clouds all produce good sunsets. Mountainous coastlines break up the clouds, as on the West Coast of Scotland, and help ensure this type of weather condition on many evenings.

A wide-angle lens will only make a good sunset when you have water or a reflective foreground to expand the scale of the shot. The light from the sun should also extend well into the sky; in short, the kind of sky-filling sunset which would make anyone stop and look.

Opposite: a blood-red sunset aided by a graduated filter and minimal exposure with an 80–200mm zoom lens, by *Alan Blair*.

Left: both foreground and background detail make this sunset more than just a disc in the sky. Photograph by *R. L. Driver*.

Below: a sunset does not have to include the sun, when suffused colour can imply it so well in this telephoto seascape by *Bernard Child*.

A telephoto lens is much more useful for inland sunsets and those days when a lonely red disc sinks down without much sign or colour in the clouds or atmosphere. A 135mm lens enlarges the sun enough to show acceptably in a postcard sized print. A 200mm is far better, and gives the right impression to match the sunset as seen by our eyes. Lenses of around 400–600mm produce a sun which is apparently much bigger, and begins to look like those film sequences and posters which show huge red balls suspended behind silhouetted leopards on branches! The actual size of the sun, on film, is about 1mm for each 100mm of lens focal length – a 50mm lens makes a sun image about .5mm wide, a 500mm lens makes one about 5mm in diameter or nearly one quarter of the height of a 35mm landscape shot. With a 2000mm lens the sun effectively 'fills the frame'.

You have probably been warned not to look at the sun through a telephoto lens. This is to some extent true, because looking through a very fast telephoto fitted to a camera with a special focusing screen on a bright day could damage your eyes seriously. Any sunset which looks colourful enough to photograph is not going to harm your eyes if looked at directly, let alone through the camera, with its focusing screen to intercept all direct rays.

Telephoto lenses are not like binoculars because you do not see directly through them. It is perfectly safe to focus through any normal lens and camera on the setting sun, and to take a meter reading or use auto exposure.

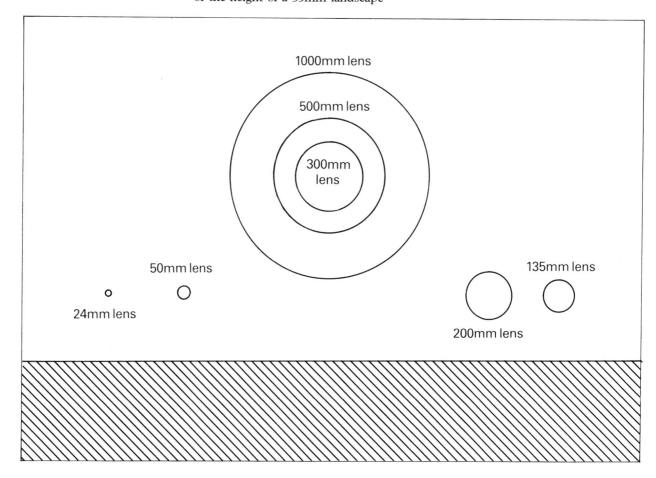

Above: compared to the outline of a 35mm film frame, the circles show the actual size of the sun as given by different focal lengths of camera lens. **Right:** do not dismiss black and white for sunsets – with careful printing, they work just as well as in colour. Photograph by *David Kilpatrick.*

Right: a foreground figure and water to reflect the silhouette makes a beach sunset better. Taken using a 45–135mm zoom by *David Kilpatrick*.

Far right: with no available strong foreground, *Graeme Cathcart* found rocks to include in his composition.

Exposure is a creative control in sunset shots. Everything depends on the effect you want. Without any adjustment, automatic cameras will give normal-looking results with standard and wide-angle lenses but will tend to produce a deeper red sun than normal in a dark sky when used with long lenses. An increase of one or two stops, depending on the conditions, will restore a light orange sun in a 'bright' sky.

If the sun itself is fairly bright, and the sunset is a result of unusual clouds or dust in the air, the metering system may be strongly affected by the inclusion of the sun itself. The result

should be a deep, rich overall colour with a small very bright area for the sun. To correct this, increase the exposure by a stop ($\times 2$). On simple cameras use the backlight button if fitted, and on cameras with AE lock, meter from the scene excluding the sun and then re-compose the shot.

Sunsets can be improved by fitting a coloured graduated filter in a warm brown (tobacco) or pink shade. This will restore a weak sunset, with little colour in the sky, to a normal visual appearance. Do not use them on scenes where the sky turns bright pale blue just above the orange-yellow zone: effect would be lost.

Right: a wide-angle sunset is made brighter by deliberate over-exposure and a simple composition without heavy silhouetted details. Photograph by *Graeme Cathcart*.

Foreground interest is the one factor which really makes a sunset successful. The lighting means that most foregrounds are silhouettes, so you have to pick recognisable and distinctive shapes like trees or figures.

There is no point in using a vague form like a rock as a foreground unless it has some detail present, which can be provided by reflections from a wet surface. The shoreline makes a good foreground and if you have a tripod, a long exposure at sunset can create superb fluid effects from moving water as well.

Flash can be added to illuminate foreground subjects like driftwood as well as for shots with people in. Normally, it should be possible to point and shoot with one-touch cameras if the sunset is bright. The sky may seem a little too dark behind the flashlit figures but this is much better than a bright sky behind black shapes. With cameras like the Minolta X-500 and 7000 or the Polaroid Sun 600, the balance between the sunset sky and flash exposure is automatically calculated and should be correct. With TTL-flash cameras like the Olympus OM-2 you simply set the main exposure for the sunset, and the fill-in flash will be acceptably accurate. The general tendency in all cases like this is for a slightly over-bright foreground and it can pay to vary the settings and take a few shots.

Colour prints of sunsets are sometimes disappointing, because the effect you remember does not end up in the print. The colours look weaker and the sun much smaller. The same picture, shot on colour slide film and projected on to a normal metre-wide screen, would be much better as the colours are retained in their full splendour and the larger reproduction works well even with normal lenses. Projecting a 500mm mirror-lens sunset slide makes the sun look far too big and artificial. A 10 × 8″ print of the same slide would probably just look 'good'.

Remember that sunrise exists, too. On east-facing coasts, where the sun may set behind hills so that you never see a full sunset, it can be worth watching the weather and thinking of rising early to catch the dawn. Sunrise rarely has the same lingering colours

as sunset, but on the other hand there can be spectacular low-lying mists, frost or dew on foliage, and a general quality to the light which works well in black and white as well as colour. You also have another advantage of a rarely photographed subject!

Above: *Chris Mole* used a telephoto lens, a direction diffusion filter and an orange filter to create a sunset image from ordinary daytime light, concealing the sun itself behind the pier architecture.

USING FLASH

Over half the pictures taken by family photographers and beginners are with flash, because the camera comes out at family gatherings, parties and events. This is a pity in some ways. With a flash fitted to the camera, most of the ideas about lighting and techniques are simply passed by. The picture is a result of the composition, the subject and a harsh form of direct lighting.

Sometimes direct flash looks very good. Newspaper 'paparazzi' snatching glimpses of the famous know that some of their flash-on-camera pictures are as glamorous as carefully-lit studio shots, highlighting eyes, teeth and hair most successfully. Others look dreadful, as any red-faced businessmen snapped at a dinner will confirm; complexions look like orange-peel or whitewash and the room in the background like a cave. In general terms, flash shots look good in small, light rooms with the camera a reasonable distance from the subject. The closer you get with the flash, and the bigger or darker the surroundings, the harsher the result will be.

Flash with wide-angle lenses is prone to several problems. The average flashgun will cope with lenses down to 35mm focal length, or 28mm when fitted with a diffusing lens over the flash. Some will also cover the field of view of a 24mm lens with a special attachment. At close distances with lenses of around 28mm, the centre of the subject will be much closer to the flashgun than the edges. The lens already tends to be a little brighter in the middle of the picture than the corners, and the flash has the same sort of characteristics. Spreading light over an angle of about 90° from a virtual point source is not easy.

Wide-angle flash shots therefore tend to get darker in the corners, and if the subject is centrally positioned and close to the camera, it may be too brightly lit in proportion. As you need to get closer with wide-angles, this brings the flash nearer to the front members of a group of people. In proportional terms, it does not move as much towards the 'second row' of people standing behind. This means the front row gets more light than the back row, and you end up with some light faces and some too dark.

There are easy ways out of this.

First of all, don't use a wide-angle unless you have to, and then use it for shots like a whole room with people further away, not for close-ups. Secondly, arrange your groups in a line at about the same distance from the camera all round. Make a slight curve or a dished line, not a straight line – then the faces will all be evenly illuminated. Instead of a second row behind the first, get some of your group to squat down so that they are between the others and their faces are lower down. It also fits the shape of a print better.

Flash shots with a standard 50mm lens are often better than those with a one-touch camera (fitted with a 35–40mm lens) for these reasons. If you can possibly shoot with a longer lens, like a zoom set to 70mm, you will find that flash portraits and small groups indoors are much better. The lighting is very much more even.

Red eye is a familiar phenomenon where the pupils of the eyes shine a bright red whenever flash is used. It only happens with some cameras and flash units and is unpredictable.

To avoid red eye, the flash should be moved away from the lens of the camera. You can not do this with most one-touch models, and red eye then occurs whenever the room is fairly dark and the subject looks directly at the camera. With 35mm SLRs, the flash may already be about 15cm above the lens because the body of the flashgun goes between the camera and the flashtube itself. This can be enough to cure red-eye totally.

If not, try fitting the camera with a handgrip that holds the flash (using an extension cord) to one side. Red eye will disappear but strong shadows will be cast to the opposite side of the subject, and care must be taken to arrange groups or pairs of people so that the shadow does not fall across a face.

Removing the flash entirely from the camera and holding it by hand, you can create an angle of about 45° between the light source and subject, which produces a stronger modelling and reveals shape and texture. The problems are once again to do with shadows, and with your own accuracy in aiming the flash; fit it with a wide-angle diffuser to minimize any errors.

Computer flash works out the exposure automatically, with a choice of aperture settings for the film speed in use. You set the filmspeed on the flash dial, set the control for a particular f-stop, and then set this f-stop on the camera lens. The flashgun has an exposure sensor which cuts off the light as soon as the subject has received the correct level of illumination. As long as the aperture set on the camera is the same as the one on the flashgun, the exposure will be correct.

Different computer flash units have widely varied specifications. The *GN*, or guide number, is a figure which expresses the power of the flash – a metric guide number of 30 (at filmspeed ISO 100) is considered normal for more expensive flashguns, 20 would be suitable only for direct flash fairly close-up, and 60 is the kind of power only a professional really needs. Anything between 28 and 40 should be adequate for shots taken inside ordinary domestic surroundings with a 35mm SLR. The GN is actually the aperture the flash would need at a certain distance, multiplied by the distance itself, so that GN 28 means a flash would need f2.8 at 10 metres distance.

You can use this information to compare different flashguns, to work out how far away you can shoot at night, and to check up on your settings. Just divide the guide number by the distance in metres (for a metric GN) or feet (for a 'ft' GN, often quoted) and you end up with the correct aperture to set. Thus:

Distance – 2.5 metres
GN of flash for ISO 100/m – 32
Aperture to set = 32 divided by 2.5
Result: 12.8

Set the aperture between f11 and f16, as this is closest to 12.8. If in doubt always set the next larger aperture, which would in this case be f11, as manufacturers do tend to overstate the GNs of their flash units by half a stop!

Manual flashguns, and the manual settings on computer guns, have a dial or scale on the back which does this calculation for you. You set an arrow to the filmspeed, and then read off the correct aperture against a distance scale in feet and metres. This is more reliable than your own calculation because the dial automatically uses the correct GN for the filmspeed and the flashgun.

The manual setting is always the full output of a flashgun unless there is a separate control for manual operation at fractional outputs like 1/2 power, 1/4, 1/8 and 1/16th. The main use for these low-power settings is when you have an auto-winder or motordrive fitted. A flash at full power, with fresh batteries, takes anything from 4 to 10 seconds to recycle between each shot unless you are very close and work on automatic operation. Sports and action shots are hardly ever close-ups, and the background of a large stadium does not help accurate automatic exposure. On 1/4 power manual, a flash can be made to keep up with a 1.5 or 2 frames per second winder, and on very low powers like 1/8 or 1/16, it will shoot at 3.5 or 5 frames per second for short bursts.

Remote sensor flashguns are computer flash models which have a sensor cell that can be unplugged, and fitted to a camera-top hot shoe which links up to the flash with a cable. The result is that the sensor cell always aims at the subject, from the camera position, regardless of what you do with the flash unit. Normally the cell aims forwards from the front of the flashgun.

With remote sensor guns, the fractional power manual settings are often provided by the remote module even if not a feature of the gun itself. It may also be possible to link two guns to a single sensor cell and control a multiple-lighting set up.

Dedicated flashguns, of any type, are simply units which connect electronically to a particular camera – or several types, with a switch to change makes. The simplest dedicated guns switch the camera's electronic shutter to the correct flash synchronisation setting, and do no more. The next common feature is a 'flash ready to fire' light which blinks in the viewfinder, so that you can keep the camera to your eye and not have to check up. Better systems add a flash check light in the viewfinder which only lights up if the subject has received correct exposure, and also read the filmspeed off the camera's

own meter setting, eliminating the possiblity of having the wrong filmspeed set on the flash. The ultimate basic refinement in dedicated flash (for shutter priority SLRs) also sets the lens aperture to match the computer setting selected.

X synchronisation is simply a term for the correct setting of any camera shutter so that the flash fires at the precise moment that the shutter is fully open. On one-touch cameras, this usually sets the shutter back to 1/250 as soon as the flash is turned on. On 35mm SLRs, the X speed depends on the type of shutter used and can by anything between 1/30 (very old cameras) and 1/250 (normally only found on cameras with a top shutter speed of 1/4000). The most common X speeds are 1/60 for cameras with a cloth shutter, and 1/90 to 1/125 for those with a metal shutter. If the X speed is also a standard shutter speed like 1/60, it will probably just be marked in green or red on the shutter dial to remind you which speed to set. If it is an unusual speed like 1/90, then

it will probably be marked as a separate X setting at one end of the shutter speed scale, beyond 1 second or 1/1000. Even when this is the case, you can normally use any speed *longer* than the X speed for flash combined with a time exposure – for example, flash plus 1 second to catch a sunset behind a flashlit portrait. You must never use speeds *shorter* than the X speed.

If you do, part of the frame will be missed off, so that a black section appears to cover an area in each photograph. If the X speed is 1/60, setting 1/125 and using flash will result in a picture which is only half there, because the shutter will cover half the film at the moment the flash fires. Remember that an electronic flash may have a duration of anything between 1/1000 and 1/50,000 of a second and the timing of this instant is very important.

One complaint against dedicated flashguns which set the shutter speed, as nearly all do, is that you can not over-ride the X speed set. On the other hand, these guns normally return the camera to normal operation in the intervals between shots when the flash is still charging itself up, so that if you fire rapidly you get some natural exposures and some flash exposures, all correct, with automatic switching between the two. Some cameras, like the Minolta X-500, allow you to change the shutter speed even when using dedicated flash so that natural light and flash can be freely combined. The similar X-300 model at a lower price does not.

TTL-OTF is a term used to describe through-the-lens, off-the-film flash exposure reading. This is the ultimate form of dedicated flash, and links the gun totally to the camera. A light sensor inside the camera body picks up the image from the surface of the film during the flash exposure itself, and terminates the light output from the flash at the precise instant that the film has received enough exposure. Flashguns like this are available for Contax, Pentax, Nikon, Rolleiflex, Minolta, Olympus and other cameras. The camera must have the necessary system built-in the enable it to function. TTL-OTF is the most accurate form of flash and can be used for anything from night-time photography to microscope exposures.

Bounce flash is simply a technique for aiming the flash at a convenient white or neutral coloured surface, such as the ceiling, instead of directly at the subject. The bounce surface should be in a suitable position to act as a 'light source' of the resulting diffused, reflected light. A very low ceiling, close to the subject, is not suitable; both photographer and subject then have to sit down rather than stand.

Flash units with a fixed sensor cell aiming from the front of the gun may have a swivelling, tilting flash-head which enables bounce operation without removing the gun from the camera. Remote sensor units often still have this feature, for convenience, but do not necessarily need it as the entire unit can be aimed in any direction once the sensor cell is attached to the camera and not the flash. TTL-OTF flashguns have the same advantage, combined with totally accurate reading of the complex results which can be produced by linking two or three flashguns on cables and mounting them on tripod stands to bounce off ceilings, walls, white sheets of card or special umbrella-style flash reflectors.

Twin tube flashguns have a second small flash-head positioned below a tilting and swivelling main head, aiming permanently at the subject. With these, the ceiling height and the exact direction and position (or even colour) of the bounce surface is not very important, because half the light is direct flash. This direct flash is weak enough not to create strong shadows, but strong enough to even out the general diffused eye and chin shadows created by ceiling bounce flash.

Attachments available for flash units include reflectors, bounce cards which fit above the flash when mounted on the camera, diffusers for extreme wide angle photography, coloured filters for effects lightings, and telephoto adaptors to create a narrow angle beam of light for use with long lenses. Most flashguns take either two or four size AA (MN 150) 1.5v batteries, and those that take four are nearly always a better proposition all round than their smaller cousins. Some expensive models have optional mains operation, rechargeable built-in batteries, or high

Opposite top: a single camera-top flashgun, removed from the hot shoe using an extension cord, was placed under this sea-urchin on a glass table-top by *S. Higgins* for a very effective but simple slide.

Opposite bottom: two flashguns were needed for this picture of a dyed ostrich feather on a small offcut of blue perspex sheet. One was on the camera; the second, just underneath the perspex on an extension cable. By having the perspex at a slight angle, reflections back were avoided. Photographed with a 70–210mm zoom lens on macro. By *David Kilpatrick*.

Above: using nothing more than a glass table-top, tracing foil and a single camera-type flashgun, *Mike Travers* produced this still life which rivals many professional studio results. He used Kodachrome film and a 35mm SLR. The short duration of the flash exposure freezes the bubbles.

power packs which you wear over your shoulder and can allow 500 or more flashes in a single recharging.

Flash exposure

Because so many pictures are taken using flash, most flashguns are now as accurate as cameras at giving correct exposure. There are two conditions which may fool the flash, or result in poor exposure. The first is when you have a pair of people, one at each side of the shot, with a space in between them (this happens with 'shake hands, take the trophy' presentation shots).

The flash sensor, even with TTL-OTF reading off the film, probably only takes the general central area of the picture into account. This is empty and dark, and the flash therefore fires at a much higher power than needed and you end up with washed-out faces. The solution is to avoid an empty area dead centre in the picture or position your two subjects in front of a neutral curtain, wall or other backdrop.

The second flash problem is with bounce flash. Often, the contrast of the lighting is reduced by bounce flash operation to an extent where the whole picture seems rather grey. This can be combined with slight under-exposure to produce a very dull result. Twin tube flash overcomes this. Normally, it is safe to allow a little extra exposure for bounce flash shots; if the flashgun has an f4 setting, use between f2.8 and f4 on the camera. Always use the *widest* aperture available with bounce – given a choice between f8 and f4 at ISO 100, pick f4 and never use f8 for bounce. Reserve the smaller lens opening for direct flash.

Fill-in flash when not available as an automatic function on the camera is a hard nut to crack. The idea is that you increase the detail visible in dark shadows facing the camera by firing a controlled flash into them, which will have no effect on a distant brightly lit background. With a 35mm SLR, the immediate problem is the synchronisation or X speed: if it is limited to 1/60, and you have ISO 200 film in the camera, the correct exposure would be 1/60 at f32 in bright sun. Your flashgun probably does not have a setting anywhere near f32 even if your lens does.

First of all, you should use a slow

film when expecting to use fill-in flash outdoors in sunshine. Do not exceed ISO 100. A camera with an X speed of 1/125 is a great help, and so is a zoom lens. The zoom enables you to vary your shooting distance so that the required aperture for flash can be adjusted. The flash should operate, or be set, for a lens opening about one stop wider than the actual stop you are using; if your camera is set to 1/125 at f/11 with ISO 64 film, set the flash for f8 on computer operation, or adjust your distance so that the flash would need f8.

Variable manual power flash units are as useful here as zoom lenses, and cameras with X speeds up to 1/250 greatly extend the possibilities, because you then have 1/60, 1/125 and 1/250 to choose from when selecting your aperture and shooting hand-held pictures.

This technique is also called synchro-sun, and despite very many explanations most photographers find

it hard to use. The key is to remember that your flash must never provide more exposure than the existing daylight, or the subject ends up being a bright cut-out against a darker background which looks like a stage set or a bad Hollywood movie. If in doubt, give less flash than you think right; set the flash for f5.6 when the lens is at f11.

There is another kind of flash photography, which gives you much greater control, and opens up a whole new range of pictures in its own right. This is photography with your own home studio – not as ambitious an idea as it sounds, requiring minimal space, and surprisingly easy to tackle.

Below: using fill-in flash or synchro sunlight technique. **Below left:** the picture in normal lighting, without any flash. **Lower left:** too much flash has been added, deliberately, to show the way in which the fill-in lighting works. **Right:** the final shot has balanced fill-in flash and soft focus provided by an 85mm Varisoft Rokkor lens. Photographs by *David Kilpatrick*.

THE HOME STUDIO

The idea of a studio, on any level, is to produce controllable lighting and set the subject against an appropriate background. Because electronic flashguns produce light instantaneously, you can not judge the effect of positioning them or changing their power.

With experience, you may want to produce better portraits and set up abstract or still life pictures. A home studio lighting kit, unpacked from a case and assembled for temporary use in a living room, can help you do this.

Modelling lights

The first step to previewing and controlling light is to see it. A tungsten (continuous) light attached to a flash is called a 'modelling' light because it lets you see how the light 'models' the subject. Modelling lights can be separate, or built-in to the flash.

If you already own two or more battery flashguns, modelling lamp assemblies with brackets to hold these can be bought at low cost. The mains-powered lamps can be fitted with different wattage bulbs to match the relative GNs of your flashguns.

You can use the fixed relationship between the modelling lamps and the flash guns to work out exposure as well as lighting. To do this, you have to make some test shots to find out the right flash exposure at (for example) three metres distance. Then, with the curtains drawn to exclude any other light, you take an exposure meter reading from the modelling lights for exactly the same set up.

Let's say your flash needs f8 at ISO 100/21°. You set ISO 100/21° on your meter, and take a reading. The meter shows that at f8 you would need a one-second exposure. You know now that if you take a reading for the f-stop required at a one second exposure, it will equal the correct flash exposure. You will not actually TAKE your picture with a one-second shutter speed, you are just using it as a reference point to find the flash f-stop.

Battery powered flash guns can take up to 15 seconds to recycle between every shot when used with mains adaptors. Mains flash units of similar power to larger battery models take 1 or 2 seconds and have modelling lamps built-in. Simple models have

Above: modelling lights enable the photographer to direct the model's pose so that the effect is correct. Photograph by *Adrian Bassett.*

Opposite: flash can be held next to a lamp in a holder to make up your own studio lighting outfit.

fixed flood reflectors and a single power setting. More expensive ones have interchangeable reflectors and half power or other reduced output settings, combined with a higher maximum output.

You should need no more than three flash heads. Portraits can be taken with just one flash and a reflector panel. Two flash heads give more control. If you still have your battery-powered gun as well, it can be used in combination with studio mains units for some effects like hair lighting.

Because flash can be harsh, special diffusers, reflecting umbrellas and soft dish reflectors are made. The most versatile reflector is a white nylon umbrella which can be used to bounce the flash off, or aim it through. Either way the light reaching the subject is softened, with smooth tones and soft shadows.

To control the light and judge it exactly, you must set up your home studio in a room with heavy curtains so there is very little natural light.

Turn the room lights off after the modelling lamps have been turned on. Then you will see just where shadows fall, whether there are shiny reflections on faces, and which angle gives the best effect.

The flash will need stands, which are simple poles with a tripod base and adjustable height. Useful extras include a reflector sheet which is also mounted on a stand and can be moved round to bounce back some of the light to fill in shadow areas, and a background holder on a stand which will take rolls of special heavy paper in various colours for portrait backdrops.

Think of your home studio when you decorate rooms. Plain wallpaper, with an area around 1 × 1.5m free from marks, can make a good basic backdrop. Plain velvet floorlength curtains in a warm, muted colour are also ideal. Plain or random carpets, goatskin or sheepskin rugs, and furniture without bright colours or strong patterns can also be used.

Space requirements

For portraits, a room at least 3 × 4 metres (9 × 12ft) is required. To photograph two or three people together, a length of 5 metres or 15ft; for full length shots, 6 metres or 18ft. Small products, babies and pets can often by photographed in much smaller rooms. In many rooms you do not need reflectors or umbrellas; you can bounce the flash off white walls and ceiling, and judge the effect by eye.

Flash exposure meters

Calculations, tables, and using the camera's TTL meter for flash exposure judging are not ideal methods. The best solution is a flashmeter. This works like a normal hand-held exposure meter, but it is aimed from the subject position towards the camera. Pressing a button on the meter fires the flash via the normal synchro cable, and an instant reading is taken. Most flash meters indicate the required f-stop without any further scales or dials to set. Some meters combine both daylight and flash reading capabilities, and some are suitable for cable-less operation.

Below: a small background created in vivid colours from silk flowers and trellis provides an ideal domestic studio portrait setting, lit with two flash units and a gold reflector panel. Photograph by *David Kilpatrick.*

BASIC LIGHTING SET-UPS

Single direct flash

Direct flash on the camera gives flat, harsh results and throws hard shadows on the background. To show facial shape and eliminate the background shadow, position the flash at about 45° above and to one side. Make sure both eyes are lit. The nose shadow should not cross the mouth or cheek.

Single umbrella flash

This is the same arrangement, but instead of aiming directly at the subject, the flash is turned away in the opposite direction to bounce off an umbrella reflector. The nose shadow is softer, the face tones smoother, and positioning is much less critical.

Adding a reflector

A one metre square white reflector panel has been added on the opposite side of the subject from the flash, at waist-level, bouncing stray light back to lighten the face shadows. This improves the shot considerably, without needing an extra flash. A silver reflector gives a stronger effect.

Adding a hairlight

Outside the camera's view, a small flashgun positioned above or behind the subject on the opposite side from the main light puts a glancing shine into the hair. To create an all-round halo when the subject has fine hair, the flash can be hidden directly behind his or her head as in this shot.

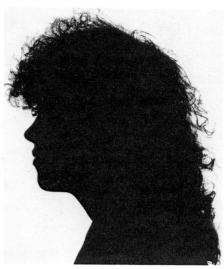

Using a fill light

For more control and even lighting, with hardly any shadows, the reflector can be replaced by a flash unit positioned very close to the camera on the opposite side from the main light, and slightly elevated. This can use an umbrella, or shine through a diffusing sheet. It should be about half the power of the main light.

Silhouette lighting

Using a plain white backdrop a metre or more behind the sitter, aim your flash units from either side at the background, keeping all light off the sitter. Base the exposure on the background. In colour, use a coloured backdrop instead. Focus on the sitter's silhouette in profile.

Male portrait lighting

When the subject is a man with a rugged skin texture, beard or 'character' looks, return to the direct flash (without umbrella or diffuser) as the main light, relieving the solid shadows with a fill light at half or quarter power. This will lighten but not soften the textural rendering.

Half profile lighting

Using a dark background and photograping in semi-profile, position a single direct flash behind the subject to one side, aiming across the subject's face towards the camera. Only one side of the face should be lit. This lighting shows up character and looks dramatic.

Rim lighting

Position the flash unit beyond the sitter, so that it can not be seen. Use a dark background and minimum exposure for a more dramatic result. The light will catch the surface of hair and skin. Rim lighting can be combined with a fill light for a less dramatic effect in glamour portraits.

Footlight effect

A theatrical or ghostly result can be obtained by placing the flash at ground level, between the camera and the sitter, aiming up at his or her face. The inverted shadows (which can be cast sharply on a close background) change faces entirely. This is not a flattering kind of lighting set-up!

Spotlighting

If you are able to control the light from a direct flash by using a cardboard tube, spotlight attachment, tele-flash attachment or optical spotlight, 45° single lighting can be turned into spotlighting. As no light is thrown on the background the effect is cleaner and brighter.

Beauty lighting

Using two flash units with two identical umbrellas or diffusers, position them very close to the subject on either side of the camera, leaving just enough room to aim the lens through the space left. There should be no shadows, but a hint of face-shape modelling remains and eyes look particularly bright. A very flattering light.

Home studio examples. **Top left:** a toadstool close-up abstract by *Mike Travers* uses a double exposure. **Top right:** a macro lens on bellows allowed this shot by *Andreas Vogt*. **Below left:** a glamour shot sandwiched with a slide of wood grain, by *M. Barnard*. **Below right:** a double exposure using a lemon and a champagne bottle, by *Richard Bradbury*.

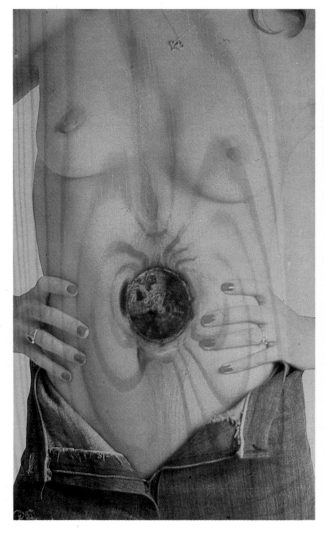

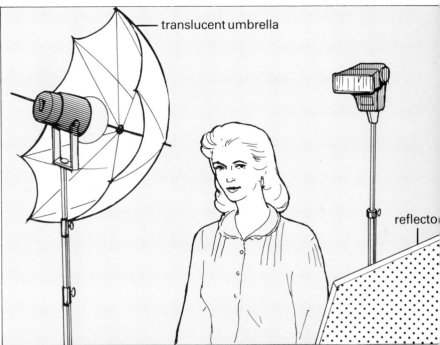

translucent umbrella

reflecto

Top: traditional portrait lighting can be simple, using only a single main light and hair-light, as in this shot by *Les Bayes*.

Lower left: this glamour portrait by *David Kilpatrick* still uses just one light, with a sheet of perspex and three colour filters.

Right: a single large diffused light source is ideal for traditional still life. Photographed for Heritage Music by *Andreas Vogt*.

Texture lighting

A single direct flashgun is ideal for 'skim' lighting when the subject is fairly flat. Fabrics, carvings, leaves, and other strongly textured subjects work well in this light. Position the flash to one side, very low down, so that it is only 5–10° above the subject. The cast shadows can make interesting shapes, too.

Backlighting

This technique can not be used with portraits, but can be used with figure studies. The single, direct light is positioned out of shot above and behind the subject, like a hair-light. The light picks out the texture and sheen of surfaces just as backlight does outdoors. It works very well with wet, textured or shiny surfaces.

Trans-illumination

Obtain a sheet of opal glass or white translucent plastic, and make it into a table-top with room to position the flash about 75–100cm below it. Photograph translucent subjects like flowers, glassware, leaves, feathers, or thin slices of fruit lit only from behind.

Floods, flash and connections

If you use black and white, or a colour slide film intended for tungsten studio lights, you can use powerful 'photoflood' tungsten lamps instead of flash. They consume more power, can become hot, and the bulbs last from 2–4 hours each only. To get small f-stops, long exposure times may be needed, calling for a tripod.

Battery flashguns, unlike floods or mains flash units which fire automatically in synchronisation, may need either small 'slave' cells to fire those remote from the camera, or a system of connectors and cables to link them to the main flash.

THE HOME DARKROOM

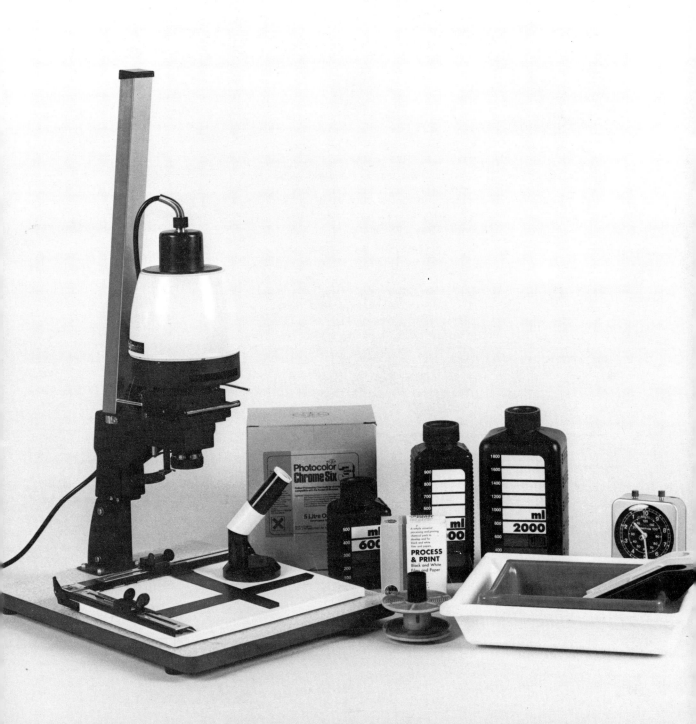

THE HOME DARKROOM

Below: a typical daylight developing tank comprises a basic 'tub', with a central cylinder on to which a film reel is placed, and then secured with a clip. The funnel-shaped main lid drops on to this and seals off all light. An agitating rod allows you to rotate the reel in the solution from outside, and a watertight cap allows you to invert the tank for strong agitation.

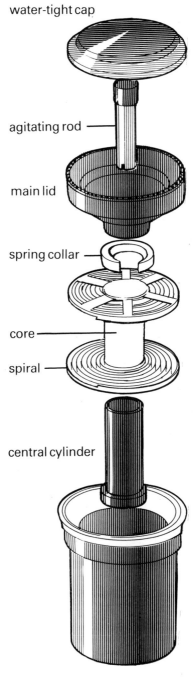

water-tight cap

agitating rod

main lid

spring collar

core

spiral

central cylinder

If you enjoy almost any other form of art, craft, DIY, or technical skill – even cookery – then there is some kind of photographic processing which will interest you.

Some processes call for a scientific approach, with accurate time and temperature control and the ability to follow instructions precisely. Others are more creative, relying on judgment as well as technical skill. Some can be done in a kitchen; others need a purpose-converted darkroom.

All photographic processing calls for a room where you can work uninterrupted, for periods of half an hour or so. Most processes need reasonable ventilation, comfortable room temperature, and hot and cold running water. Print-making needs a room which can be blacked out, but there are special tents and collapsible cupboards available for those with limited space.

The easiest places to convert are bathrooms or kitchens, because they have running water. A garden shed, cellar or large closet can be used if dry and heatable.

Film processing

Film processing, for negatives or slides, needs a lightproof *developing tank* into which the film is loaded and sealed for processing. The principle is that the exposed but invisible image on the film is developed or turned into a visible image, and then the remaining light-sensitive compounds are removed.

35mm film must be removed from its cassette in the dark, without handling the surfaces. To make life easy try to rewind your films so that a small amount of leader sticks out; mark this or tear it off to identify used films. Some cassettes are easily opened; others require a can opener to prise the end off if the film is totally rewound. Cartridge films have to be opened by breaking the plastic cartridge. Rollfilms are unwound and detached from their paper backing (a task for those with experience only).

Any and all of these operations must be done in the dark, and that means TOTAL dark. It is not enough to draw curtains or do it at night.

Loading without a darkroom

The easy solution to loading film into a developing tank is a changing bag. This is a lightproof double-skinned zipped pouch, large enough to hold films, scissors, developing tank parts and your hands inserted through elasticated lightproof cuffs.

After dark, you can probably make do with a cupboard or work under bedclothes to load a film. Be careful, wherever you load film, to avoid dust and humidity. Practice first with an old film to avoid muddle and sweaty hands which can mark the negatives.

Tank loading

Modern developing tanks have a spiral reel, into which the film slides. Oscillating the two halves of the reel makes the film feed in. Any trace of moisture may make it stick and buckle up, so reels have to be dried thoroughly and kept in a warm, dry place like an airing cupboard. After initial 'dummy film' practice, most people master loading developing tank reels easily. The reel holds the film securely and makes sure no two surfaces ever touch or stick together in the processing solutions.

The spiral reel fits over a central pillar, which is then dropped (reel to the bottom) into a cylindral drum. This is the tank body. A lid is finally place on the drum top and locked. Some designs use a push fit, others a bayonet, and others a screw thread. This completes the light-seal.

Some tanks take two or more spiral reels on the column. The normal maximum is five 35mm films in one tank. With larger models, the reels may be secured with a clip when fewer than the maximum number are used, so that they do not slide up and down the pillar during processing.

Two accessories complete the assembly. They are a cap, and a rod. The rod fits down the central hole in the lid and engages the column, so that you can twist the reel round in the solution. The cap fits over the hole in the tank lid so that it can be turned upside down even when full, without leaking. Both these devices allow you to *agitate the film* during processing, or keep the solutions moving round the film.

Without agitation, processing chemicals would stagnate and their byproducts cause uneven development. Agitation replaces worn-out solution close to the film emulsion with fresh chemicals. Agitation with the *rod*, twisting the reel round in short, sharp jerks both clockwise and anti-clockwise, is usually either ten seconds each minute end, five seconds each thirty seconds, or continuous. *Inversion agitation* with a watertight tank cap fitted means turning the tank upside down, waiting for a second, then returning it. This is 'one inversion'. Instructions usually state how many inversions and when – five inversions at the end of each minute, one inversion every fifteen seconds, or whatever.

Pouring

A pouring hole in the light-trapped main lid of the tank allows it to be filled with solutions quickly and evenly. It is normal to give the tank a couple of sharp knocks, or twist the reel with the agitation rod a few times, to dislodge any air bubbles from the film.

Pouring out is done from the outer rim of the tank, through a light-trapped seal. It should be done as rapidly as possible, and the tank should be given two or three brief circular shakes when inverted at the end of pouring to help drain off any surplus solution.

Timing and temperature

All processing times begin after the solution is fully poured in, and end when it is fully poured out. Allow 15 seconds for pouring out and draining the tank. Most processes need you to keep the temperature of each solution to within 1°C of a stated figure; colour processes often demand within half or quarter of a degree. The figures stated always mean the *average* temperature throughout the processing in any one solution. This is not the same as the starting temperature, unless you can keep your tank body immersed in a water-bath maintained at the correct temperature. In air, heat is always lost unless you warm up the tank from time to time. Keeping the room 2°C warmer than the solutions also avoids cooling.

Monitored processing means doing just this, with a thermometer inserted in the tank every half-minute or so, and a hot water bath to hand for correcting falls in temperature. *Drift* processing is easier; if the stated temperature is 20°C and the process time ten minutes, you start at 21°C. after five minutes, you measure the temperature; if it is 20°C, then you do nothing, as it will probably drop to 19°C so that the average will be exactly 20°C over the ten minutes. If it is lower, you then apply a little warmth, to bring it back to 20°C, and try to hold it there. Processing thermometers, whether traditional spirit and mercury, column or dial types, give reliable (certified) measurements to within 1/4 of a degree C if required.

Flexibility

Some chemical kits tell you that you can compensate for lower temperatures with longer process times, and vice-versa; many have tables. At first stick to 'target' temperatures and times; later you will find the data on variations useful for exact control.

A basic outfit for developing your own films, including black and white chemicals: A – a universal developing tank, which must be loaded in the dark but can be used in daylight once closed: B – a measuring cylinder; C – a photographic thermometer; D – developer concentrate; E – fixer concentrate; F – a washing hose; G – a film wiper; H – clips to hang the film up to dry after wiping off excess water.

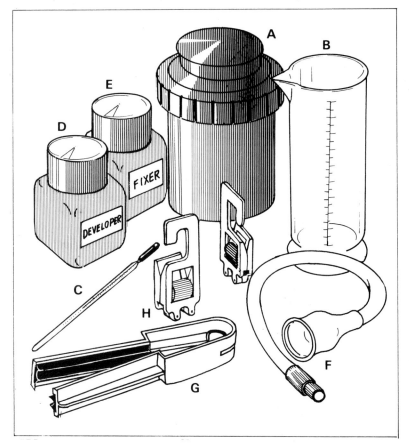

Even in very critical colour processes, only some of the solutions and steps need to be exact. The final wash in running water which most films need is not so precise. However, your tap-water in winter may be around 12°C or less. You will need water of at least 16°C and probably 24°C. Do not try to mix this from hot and cold supplies. It is better to keep a bucket, make up several litres, and follow the instructions for washing or rinsing in a *series of baths* rather than running water.

Solution mixing

Very few photo processing solutions come ready to use. They may be powders which are dissolved, concentrates which are diluted, or a combination of both. You do not need distilled water, but a photo filter system can be very useful to ensure that dirt from the tap does not damage films. Solutions which can be used several times should also be filtered. In very hard or soft water areas, a demineralizer may improve results with colour processes.

Before mixing chemicals, make sure you have graduated measures – cylinder jugs with millilitre and fluid ounce markings, in sizes from 45ml to 2000ml. Wash measures thoroughly after each use to avoid cross-contamination with chemicals. Photo storage bottles in glass or plastic should be used to keep reusable working solutions; 'one-shot' solutions are thrown away after use. Plastic funnels, again washed thoroughly after use, help avoid splashes or spills when handling solutions.

Make up solutions in a ventilated room, on a non-porous worktop, away from food, children, or animals. A large print developing dish is an ideal 'tray' for solution making; so are gardeners' seed trays. Follow instructions exactly and never vary the order of dilution or mixing, or change and split quantities. Rubber gloves and a protective darkroom apron are sensible precautions when handling any photographic solutions. Your hands must be kept clean and dry for handling film and paper.

Black and white film

The simplest process to try first is black and white film processing. After the film is loaded in the tank, this takes about ten minutes, plus a running water wash which may be up to 30 minutes, and thirty minutes for the film to dry off.

The first step, an alkaline solution called *developer*, acts on crystals of silver salts in the film emulsion which have received light, turning them into metallic silver. Parts of the film where the crystals did not receive enough light are not developed in this way. The effect is proportional, so that density of black silver formed depends on the exposure received.

After the correct time is up the developer is poured out and an acid *stop bath* is poured in to halt its action. Extended development would blacken more of the emulsion than necessary. Finally, a *fixer* solution is used to remove all the remaining light-sensitive crystals which have not been developed, so that the unexposed parts of the film are clear.

The processing throughout is normally at 20°C/68°F, within 1°C either way. The developer is usually made up just before use, takes 5–12 minutes to process, and is thrown away. The stop bath (15 seconds) and the fixer (30 seconds to 3 minutes) are both made up and stored in bottles, one litre being enough for 10–15 films. After fixing, the negatives are no longer sensitive to light and can be checked. If dried now, they would deteriorate rapidly because of residues in the emulsion. These are water-soluble, and have to be washed out.

To bring the temperature down to match that of running tap water, successively cooler baths at 3°C steps should be used. Washing takes a minimum of 20 minutes at 20°C/68°F, and in colder tap water around 15°C it should be extended to at least an hour. Afterwards, the film is removed carefully from the reel, and hung up to dry in a dust-free atmosphere. Surplus water can be removed with special rubber squeegee tongs or careful use of a very soft, well soaked chamois cloth.

Opposite:

Above: to process colour negative films, you need a kit with developer, bleach-fix and possibly stablizer, a very accurate thermometer and measuring cylinders. **Left:** to bring the solutions up to temperature, use a hot water bath.

The colour developer is poured in rapidly, and the temperature checked during processing. Afterwards, it is returned to its bottle for re-use.

A tempered water rinse is followed by blix (bleach-fix), which is also stored for further use. After a running water wash, the film may be stablized for added permanence.

As soon as the film is hung up, it can be wiped down with a rubber bladed squeegee to remove excess water. This has to be done immediately, or the film will dry slightly and be damaged on wiping. After drying, it should be filed in suitable protective sleeves before printing.

Colour negative film

The steps involved in processing colour negatives, for making prints later on, are similar to black and white processing, but the temperatures involved are higher and the time and temperature control has to be much more accurate. The developer must be kept within 1/4°C and 15 seconds of the stated time. Usually, the developer takes between 4 and 5 minutes at 38°C. As well as developing a silver image as in black and white, this bath creates the dye image which forms the colours in conjunction with the silver image.

A stop bath follows, and this may also have a hardening agent which makes the film less easily scratched. The developer forms both coloured dye images, and a black silver image. The 'fixing' stage is replaced by *blix* or *bleach-fix*, which in a single bath removes the silver image to leave coloured dyes only, and then eliminates both the original unexposed emulsion and the bleached silver residues. This step takes about 8 minutes, depending on the film type.

In some processes, the blix may be followed by a wash (often shorter than for black and white, but at a much higher temperature) and then a final rinse in a stabilizer solution, which is intended to stop the colour dyes from changing. In others the stabilizer is omitted.

Colour negative chemicals come in kits which are made up to a quantity like 250ml, 1 litre or 5 litres, and stored in plastic or glass bottles (never used for any other purposes) of exactly the right capacity. A 250ml kit may process anything up to 8 films, depending on type. Only after the maximum number has been processed is the kit discarded. The working life of a kit is around six weeks, but in some amateur kits you can make up half at a time, storing the remaining concentrate for up to 6 months. This is ideal for occasional users. Some black and white films, called chromogenic, are processed in chemicals similar to those used for processing colour negatives. Ordinary colour negative kits can be used as well as purpose-made ones.

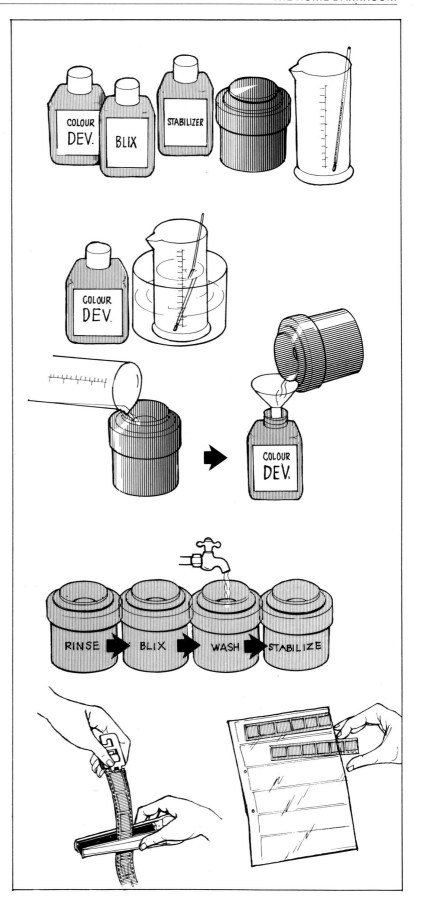

Colour slide processing

The only film process which gives you a final picture to view, without further printing, is colour slide (transparency). The slides can be viewed in strips, with a magnifier, or put through a pocket viewer, table-top viewer or projector and screen. Prints can be made from slides if needed.

Colour slide processing is similar in time and temperature stringency to colour negative processing. If anything, greater care is needed. It is possible to adjust for small errors in negative processing when printing, but a colour slide is a finished result and must be right to start with.

You will need more storage bottles to handle a slide processing kit, once again only used for this specific purpose. Most kits need four to six. Typical kit sizes are 600ml, 1 litre, 5 litres and so on. The processing takes about 30 minutes followed by brief washing and drying, and it is important to be able to devote your full attention to it for all this time, without interruption.

First developer may be used either with, or without, a pre-soak in pure water at a specified temperature. This depends on the kit. This developer produces a silver image only, with no dyes for colours, which is a negative.

After this first stage, different kits can be totally unlike each other. Some just require a rinse; others need a rinse followed by immersion in a 'reversal' bath before colour development. Older processes needed the film to exposed to a bright light-source instead of this bath. The latest kits are 3-bath E6, and the reversal is handled in the colour development stage.

Colour developer acts on the part of the film which was not affected by the first developer – the positive image. Because the negative image has already been developed, the colour developer has no action on it, and can not produce any dyes. It only acts on the complementary remaining 'reversal' image. The dyes are formed in inverse colour and density to the negative image, and this produces a positive slide in true colours and tones.

A *bleach fix* or *blix* bath then removes the metallic silver to leave only the pure colour dye image. In some kits, bleach and fix are separate baths. A typical one litre kit will handle ten 35mm 36 exposure type E6 films. The final wash in changes of water, or running water at a suitable temperature, is normally followed by a *stabilizing* solution to help the slide remain fade-free for as long as possible. When wet, the film has a milky, magenta appearance. Drying eliminates this, and the true colours appear. In the reversal process, the first developer and colour developer are the critical stages, needing exact time and temperature control. The remaining steps are not so critical.

Film speed changes can be made by varying the first development time, and other kits often have instructions for this. *Pushing* the speed by extending development makes it possible to expose at twice or four times the official ISO film speed. *Pulled* or shortened first development can halve the filmspeed but is less useful.

Above: a comprehensive kit for processing slides, in this case showing a complex process. Simplified versions are now available. The very accurate thermometer is an important part of the outfit, and slide mounts are necessary if the pictures are to be projected (rather than reversal printed).

Filing and mounting

Now, final processes can all be carried out without a darkroom. Colour slides can now be mounted in frames and put into projector magazines or slide filing boxes. Negatives can be cut up into suitable strips (of six 35mm frames, or three 6 × 6cm frames on 120 rollfilm) and inserted into filing sheets. These are special loose-leaf punched sheets made of a semi-transparent paper which does not scratch the delicate negatives, or affect them chemically. The sheets are then filed in a ring-binder, with index card dividers, for future reference. Most negative filing systems work in this way. Strips of unmounted colour slides can also be stored, waiting for you to mount them or make prints.

For the remaining (more creative) darkroom processes, of printing, you will need an enlarger and a room which can be blacked out, together with a reasonable workbench. A kitchen worktop about 2 metres long, or a temporary worktop covering the length of a bath, are both suitable.

Safelighting

Colour printing has to be done in total darkness, but to help you find your way round, luminous tabs and strips are acceptable. A luminous timing clock is essential. Colour 'safelights' are made which are supposed to provide enough light to see by, but only the most expensive of these are much use. The light from ordinary colour safelights is so dim that it takes many minutes to see even a vague idea of the surroundings. Safetorches, with confined beams, can be extremely valuable; have one to hand, for locating dropped or missing items.

In black and white, on the other hand, a fairly bright orange safe-lighting is acceptable. An orange or red lightbulb is not adequate – the colour must be precise. A 15 or 25 watt safelight for black and white will illuminate any normal size of darkroom well enough for all routine work. The light colour may be amber or orange, or red for special materials you are unlikely to use until you have considerable experience.

Electrical safety

As printing work involves an enlarger, with electric power directly to it, and may also involve motorized process units, care should be taken over arrangements. The 'wet bench' should be an area where all processing and wet stages take place, and no wires should run along or under this. The 'dry bench' should be reserved for all pre-processing stages, and all electrical wizardy. The one exception could be an electrically powered processor. Make sure your safelight and main room light are operated by pull-cords and not by toggle switches. Your hands may be wet or damp. The safety rules in a darkroom are the same as those for a bathroom.

Below: a typical darkroom plan for a 'third bedroom' in a typical house, with one addition – running water and a sink. The dry and wet bench, and paper and chemical storage areas, are kept separate. The film drying area is as far from the door as possible to avoid possible damage or incoming dust. If children are likely to come in, an inner safety blackout curtain is useful and chemicals should be stored in eye-level wall cupboards.

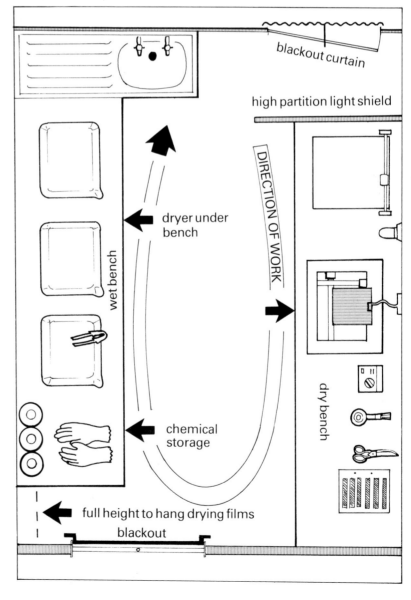

blackout curtain

high partition light shield

DIRECTION OF WORK

wet bench

dryer under bench

chemical storage

dry bench

full height to hang drying films

blackout

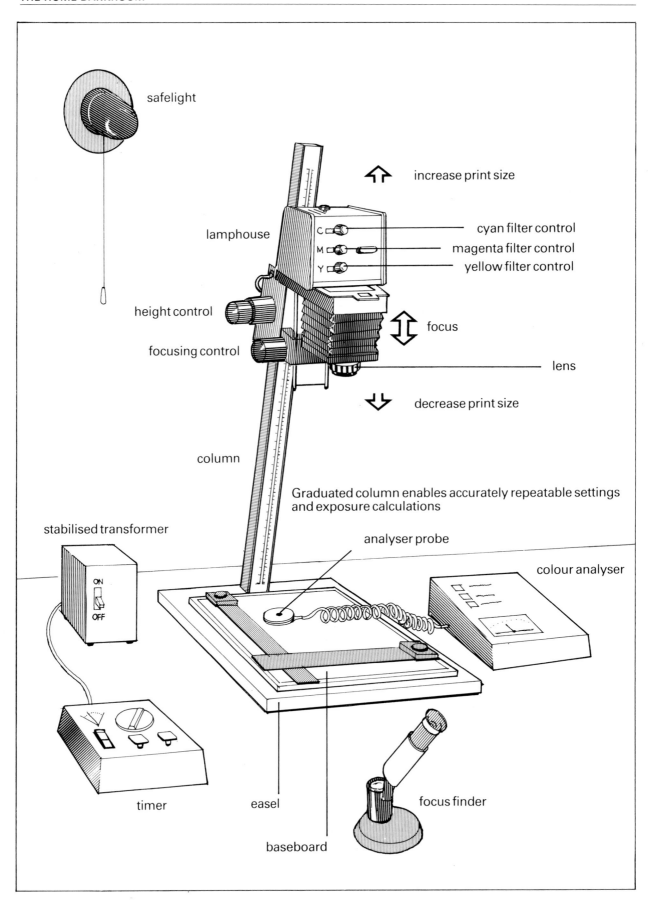

safelight

increase print size

lamphouse

cyan filter control
magenta filter control
yellow filter control

height control

focus

focusing control

lens

decrease print size

column

Graduated column enables accurately repeatable settings and exposure calculations

stabilised transformer

analyser probe

colour analyser

ON
OFF

timer

easel

focus finder

baseboard

The enlarger

Your first enlarger need not be expensive. The vital parts of an enlarger are a stage to hold the film, a light-source to illuminate it, and a baseboard and column arrangement to hold the 'head' above a sheet of printing paper.

The negative carrier, or slide holder, must obey the basic rules of the camera itself; the film should be flat, and parallel to the lens. There should be no light leaks. The simplest good arrangement consists of a film track just like the inside of a camera, with a lens focusing by a screw thread, and a flat pressure plate which keeps the film flat. Some enlargers may appear very versatile, taking several film sizes, with long bellows to focus the lens, and all kinds of interchangeable lightsources. All these features are planned so that different sizes of negative can be enlarged in one enlarger. In practice, a good 6 × 6cm enlarger is hardly ever a good 35mm enlarger too, and a good 5 × 4″ enlarger (massive) may have the ability to print both 35mm and 6 × 6cm as well but only with some inconvenience. It is only worth buying an enlarger for several film sizes if you plan to use these sizes yourself.

Black and white enlargers are fitted with a conventional tungsten bulb of 75 or 150w, mains voltage, slightly over-run for extra brightness. The light is concentrated evenly on the negative through optical condenser lenses or a diffusing box. The density of a black and white print is controlled by altering the lens aperture (brightness) and exposure time. The larger you make a print, the dimmer the projected image becomes, and the longer the exposure time needed.

To make colour prints in an enlarger like this, a further control is needed – adjustment to the colour of the light. It is fairly easy to print colour slides on a black and white enlarger, as any one make of film normally needs the same filters. A drawer fitted below the light in the enlarger allows 75 × 75mm filters to be inserted to adjust colour balance. Colour negative printing calls for more frequent changes of these filters, even within a single roll of film, and for this reason colour negatives are best printed on a special enlarger with built-in variable colour filtration.

The filters commonly used for colour printing for negatives are yellow and magenta in colour, but there is a third colour – cyan blue. This is rarely used but can be useful for slide printing. The yellow and magenta filters can also be used for changing the contrast of special black and white printing papers called Multigrade and Polycontrast, which make soft grey or hard black and white bright prints according to the colour of the printing illumination.

If colour filters were not used, a print from a colour negative would look reddish-orange. Results from slides vary, as sometimes no filters are needed for perfect prints. Multigrade black and white papers used with filtration give a slightly low contrast but acceptable print.

Colour analysers are devices to help you assess the changes you want to make in the colour of each print, to make it look natural. They do not give the correct setting straight away, but you can use them to match future negatives once you have worked out the right filters for your first print.

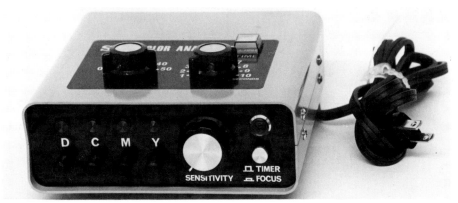

Opposite: a typical colour enlarger and accessories showing the main controls and features.

Below: a colour analyser has adjustable settings which can meter the yellow, cyan and magenta content of your negatives or slides and the time required for exposure. Some colour analysers connect directly to enlargers.

Enlarger use

The negative or slide is placed in the enlarger carrier with the emulsion side facing downwards for most printing processes. For certain processes like Ektaflex or Agfachrome-Speed, the emulsion should be upwards. Put the negative in with the bottom of the picture furthest away from you (with upright pictures, it does not matter). On the baseboard, you will probably see a blurred image when the enlarger lamp is switched on. Focus the lens to make this sharper. It is easiest to do this if you have a paper easel, or *masking frame*, in place on the baseboard. To change the size of the picture to cover the size of paper you intend to use, the enlarger head is moved up (bigger) or down (smaller). The lens has to be refocused after even the smallest change.

A *focus finder* is a kind of magnifier like a microscope in shape. Placed on the masking frame under the lens, it magnifies the image of the film-grain so much that you can focus precisely on the actual image structure.

It is easiest to focus on the masking frame with the lens at full aperture. With a focus finder, close it down two click stops. Enlarging lenses always have firm click aperture stops for use in the dark.

Once your negative or slide has been projected in this way, and composed for best effect, the enlarger is turned off. The paper is inserted in the masking frame, which holds it perfectly flat, emulsion side up. With some types of colour paper this is very hard to judge. Normally it is the side which will feel tacky if touched (on the extreme edge only) with a damp finger. The exposure is made either by timing manually, with a watch or luminous seconds timer, or using a timer wired into the circuit. A typical exposure for a 10 × 8″ print will be ten seconds with the aperture at f8. You hardly ever have to deal with times like 2 seconds or one minute unless you are making unusually large or small prints. Each printing process, from this stage on, is very different, and there are many to choose from.

Below: the masking frame is set to the size of print required, and holds the paper flat under the enlarger. The special enlarging lens (foreground) gives a very flat field and sharp focus. Most people need the help of a focus finder (on the masking easel, centre) to make full use of this quality. The blower brush removes dust from the negative, and the timer can be used for timing enlarging exposure as well as processing stages.

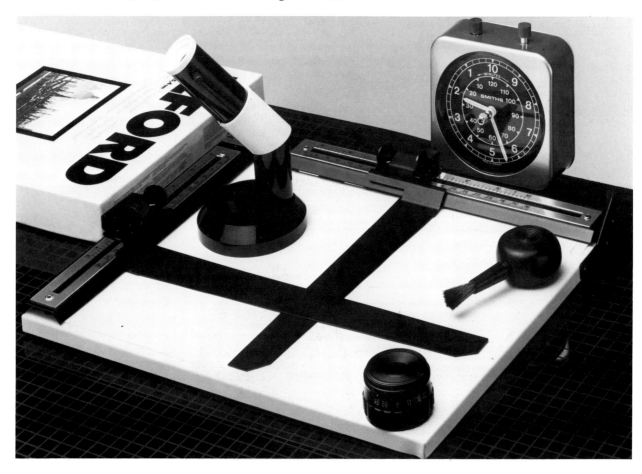

Black and white needs three dishes large enough to take the sheet of paper with room round the side to be able to move it round and lift it out using print tongs. You will also need a fourth dish or a print washing tray to wash to prints under running water. The black and white chemicals are developer, stop bath and fixer, exactly as for film processing. The normal times are 2 minutes development, 15 seconds stop bath rinse, 3 minutes fixing, 5 minutes wash and about 3–5 minutes drying in a feed-through or rack drier which uses hot air or an infra-red element.

Fibre-based black and white papers have a paper base which becomes soft in water, and may need up to an hour's washing. They can be dried at room temperature, overnight, on a rack. Heated driers take about ten minutes and can not accept many prints at a time. The disadvantages of fibre based papers are offset by exceptional quality and archival permanence.

All black and white processes are exciting because you see the image emerge, and have some control at all stages of the process. Black and white teaches you how materials react.

Left: the basic steps in processing a sheet of black and white paper using three dishes. With resin-coated quick dry papers, best results are given from hot air drying after removing excess water, but a rack can just as easily be used after blotting dry, with a 30 minute drying time at room temperature.

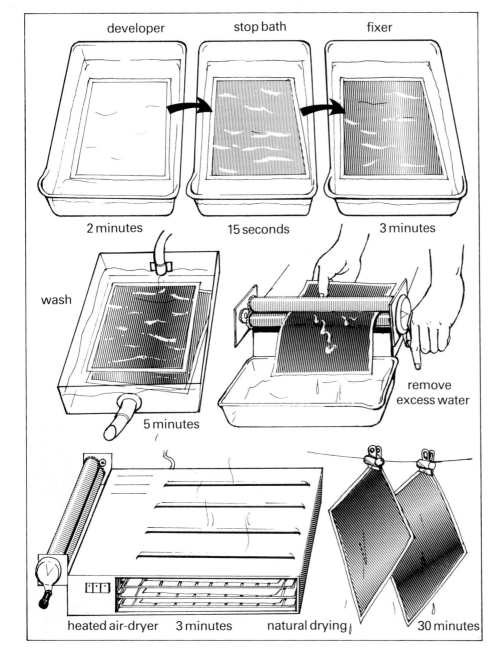

developer — stop bath — fixer

2 minutes — 15 seconds — 3 minutes

wash — 5 minutes — remove excess water

heated air-dryer 3 minutes — natural drying 30 minutes

151

A 10 × 8″ orbital processor which costs little and makes prints from colour negatives at room temperature with special easy-to-use chemical kits. It will also process black and white, and materials like Agfachrome-Speed.

Colour negative print processing is almost as quick, but more accuracy is needed. Chemicals should be fresh, equipment carefully cleaned, and instructions should be pinned up so that each step can be followed easily.

Instead of a set of dishes, you use a processor more like a film developing tank, with a lightproof cover. It is not possible to work in safelighting with colour paper. Processors may take the form of a drum or a flat tank. Once the print is placed inside, the cover is put on. At a controlled temperature, small quantities of developer, stop, and bleach-fix are poured in, agitated and discarded in turn. You can not see the print appear, but after a few minutes the lid is removed, and the colours can be judged.

Universal chemicals can be used for paper as well as film after mixing in a developer additive supplied. A test strip printer allows you to make small tests, and four 5 × 4″ prints can be fitted into most 10 × 8″ processors either for this purpose or for routine printing.

Slide printing uses the same basic processing equipment, but different processes. The Ektachrome print process uses low-cost materials but requires care in colour filtration and processing. The Cibachrome process costs more, but is more tolerant and produces very permanent, high gloss prints with exceptional colour saturation. Rapid systems like Agfachrome Speed and Ektaflex have the highest costs but can be tackled by beginners, with acceptable results and very easy room temperature processing. In theory colour slide printing is not capable of some of the very fine controls of contrast and colour you can achieve with negative printing, but most amateurs find it far easier to make a find it far easier to make a high quality print from a slide because tests can be compared with an original.

The most simplified processes do not yield exhibition quality prints, despite the claims made for them, and it is still necessary to work carefully to get the best results. There are however continual improvements in materials and methods which make tomorrow's easy processes likely to match today's state-of-the-art methods.

Large print processing

For prints larger than 10 × 8″, a processing drum is the best choice unless you have access to a professional processing machine. Drums can be used in conjunction with a water bath which also keeps the stock solution bottles and measures at the right temperature. A motor can be added to replace manual drum rotation, and a thermostat heater can easily be fitted, Dividers allow the drums to be used for smaller prints singly or in batches, and some types can be used for processing batches of colour negative film in reels.

Printing in bulk

Most amateurs processes handle a single print at a time, or half a dozen at the most. One of the easiest processing methods for making several copies is the 'deep tank line', which consists of a series of deep vertical tanks of chemicals kept at a constant temperature by thermostat. The printing paper is loaded on to a special hanger, and lowered into each bath in turn. The chemicals are not thrown away, but gradually replenished by adding fresh batches.

Print finishing

After any photographic print is made it can often be improved. Sometimes the paper shape is not correct for the picture itself, and the print should be trimmed.

To ensure a perfect rectangle and clean cuts without risk of injury, a *print trimmer* should be used. The best types have rotary cutting wheel rather than guillotine blades.

Small marks on the print from dust or hairs on the negative can be removed by *retouching* with water colour and a very fine brush. This is a technique which can be hard to master. Spotting inks intended for black and white prints can also be used to 'spot' colour prints for minor blemishes, as the difference between colour and the grey retouching ink is not noticeable. To complete the presentation, you can mount your prints either in folders available from dealers, or on board mounts using spray adhesive.

Slide viewing

Because 35mm colour slides are so small, you can not view them comfortably with the naked eye. You have to use a magnifier or a projector to enlarge the image.

Pocket viewers collapse, and assemble to form a simple magnifier with a holder for the slide. *Lupe* magnifiers have no holder and are intended to view the slide when placed on an illuminated table-top or a *slide sorter*. This is a miniature desk with a plastic top and internal lights, holding the slides on ridges in rows.

Optical viewers have a large magnifying lens and a slot at the rear, with a battery or mains illuminated panel behind the slide. You see the slide magnified, but you do not have to peer through the lens. They give a better idea of the picture impact and sharpness than a small magnifier, and several people can view in turn, with ease.

Table-top projectors with built-in screens, rather than magnifier lenses, allow several people to view the pictures at a time to size around 15 × 15cm.

Projectors throw the slide image on to a separate screen, which may be mounted on a wall, hung from the ceiling or fitted to a floor stand. The typical screen size is a little over a metre square, needing about two metres between the projector and screen. The projector also needs a table of the right height, or a stand, to keep the image centred on the screen. For true colours and brilliance, the room should be darkened. Many projectors have remote control focusing and slide change.

You can show your slides automatically, either by using a timer or a tape recorder. Timers are built into some projectors. A stereo tape recorder, used with a slide/tape synchronizer, changes the slides at pre-set moments during music or commentary.

Slide-dissolve is a method for presenting an integrated, planned sequence of slides like a film. Two projectors are used, with no sharp changes between the pictures; as one fades gradually, the next photograph replaces it.

A typical 35mm slide projector with remote control and many automatic features which allow it to be used for audio-visual presentations.

GLOSSARY

AE
Automatic Exposure – normally used to describe aperture priority operation, in which the aperture is set first and the shutter speed controlled by the AE system.

AE Lock
A button, or first pressure on the shutter release, which locks in an auto exposure reading allowing the camera to be aimed at a specific area to take the reading before re-composing the shot. Useful to take readings from the ground area, avoiding including a very bright sky.

AF
Auto focus – initials used frequently in model names for auto focus cameras.

Aperture (see f-stop)
A perforated disc or variable iris inside a lens, which can be adjusted to different diameters, and admit more or less as required. A small (narrow diameter) lens aperture gives a dim image reaching the film, a large one a bright image.

Aperture priority
See 'AE'

ASA
See Film Speed

Autofocus
A system which sets the focusing by sensing the distance from camera to subject using an electro-optical rangefinder, or a contrast sensing system reading through the camera lens.

Autowinder
A motorized film advance system which operates at two shots per second or slower, or requires pressure on the shutter to be lifted before winding on to the next shot.

B
A shutter speed marking standing for 'Brief Time' or 'Bulb' exposure. Pressing the shutter release opens the shutter; letting go closes it. B is used for exposures longer than the maximum available from the camera's shutter speed range.

Backlight
See Contre Jour

BC
An abbreviation which normally stands for 'Battery Check', found on many cameras, flashguns and other equipment.

Bellows
a) in older camera, used between lens and body to allow folding action b) in modern SLRs, fitted between lens and body to allow extremely close focusing down to almost microscope-power magnifications.

Bounce flash
A method for obtaining soft, even lighting by aiming the flash at a nearby light-coloured surface like a white ceiling, instead of directly at the subject. When mentioned in the specification for a flashgun, the term means a swivelling or tilting action of the flash head to allow this.

Cable release
A short mechanical or electrical cable which attaches to the camera, and allows shake-free release of the shutter especially when the camera is mounted on a tripod.

Camera Shake
Unsharpness caused by the camera moving during the actual exposure, especially when the shutter is open for times longer than 1/30th without a tripod.

Chrome
Term popularly used in Japan and USA to describe colour slide films.

Computer Flash
Automatic flash exposure carried out by a sensor on the flashgun, rather than through the camera lens.

Contre jour
Conditions where the main light direction comes towards the camera from behind the subject, rather than from behind the photographer.

Control back
See also Data Back. A special camera back which can be programmed to release the shutter at long intervals, after a time delay, for a fixed number of exposures, and so on. Control backs can normally switch on flashguns, imprint data, and perform motor-drive or automatic exposure bracketing functions.

Data Back
A replacement camera back which imprints the date, time, a serial number of other information on the film. Some backs also control camera functions.

Dedicated Flash
Any form of flashgun which couples through to the camera's controls when fitted, and adjusts settings automatically. The camera usually transmits lens aperture and film speed data to the flash; the flash sets the camera, in turn, to the correct shutter speed and may operate indicator lights in the viewfinder. Some systems allow off-the-film exposure control.

Delayed Action
See Self Timer

Depth of Field
At any given focus setting and f-stop, the amount of subject depth which will be apparently sharp in the final picture. Scales or guides are provided to help show this on many cameras. See Focusing and Focus.

DIN
See Film Speed

EE
A term for automatic exposure on cameras where the lens aperture (f-stop) is set automatically after the shutter has been set manually.

Ever-ready Case
A camera case which fits the camera tightly, and has a flap which can be dropped to take pictures without removing the camera. Many compact 35mm one-touch models have integral cases. Special 'ERC's are made for SLRs with zoom lenses fitted in place of 50mm lenses.

Exposure
a) A photograph or a frame of film – 'I have ten exposures left', 'Let's take another exposure'. b) the relative amount of light allowed to reach the film, through control of shutter and aperture settings ('under exposed', 'over exposed') or the actual settings used ('an exposure of 1/125 at f8').

Extension tube
A tube which fits between the lens and body on interchangeable lens cameras, in order to allow focusing at very close distances, often down to 10cm.

f-stop
A numerical expression of the lens aperture in terms of light transmitting ability. The diameter of the lens aperture divided into the lens focal length. The normal f-stop figures form a series running f1.4, f2, f2.8, f4, f5.6, f8, f11, f16, f22, f32. The same f-stop on several different lenses will always admit the same level of light.

Factorial over-ride
A control on an auto exposure camera which allows the exposure to be adjusted by a fixed factor for all shots taken while the over-ride is in use. Most over-rides can be set to x2, x4, $x\frac{1}{2}$ and $x\frac{1}{4}$ of normal exposure.

Film Speed
A numerical expression of the sensitivity of any given film to light, which is always fixed for a particular film or film type. There are three terms: ASA (obsolescent) has a scale in which doubling the number doubles the light sensitivity (e.g. 25 ASA, 50 ASA, 100 ASA). DIN (obsolescent) is a logarithmic scale in which a 3° increase in the number doubles sensitivity (15° DIN, 18° DIN, 21°DIN). The current term ISO replaces both these, and includes both numbers – ISO 25/15°, ISO 50/18°, ISO 100/21° and so on. ISO speeds can, of course, be set on meters or cameras with ASA and DIN scale markings.

Filter
A glass or plastic optical sheet which is coloured or otherwise treated to alter the appearance of a picture when placed over the camera lens. Some filters are purely corrective and intended to cut haze or deepen sky colours; others are creative, and intended to alter colours or sharpness.

Filter Thread
The threaded rim at the front of many camera lenses, which is intended to accept circular threaded filters or adaptors to fit others. This is not found on disc, autofocus 35mm, and 110 pocket.

Fisheye
A lens which takes in a field of view around 180° diagonally, and gives everything a curved or bulging appearance.

Flare
Degrading of the picture contrast by stray light. This can take the form of lower overall contrast, patches of light, or polygonal marks caused by reflection inside the lens.

Flash distance check (FDC)
A light or audio warning which sounds when an automatic flash system has given the correct exposure. Sometimes, a separate button which can be pressed to fire a flash and find out if this will be the case.

Focal Plane
The position where the film is held in the camera. Focal plane shutter: a shutter immediately in front of the film, rather than inside the lens, allowing lenses to be changed while the film is in the camera.

Focus Check
An electronic system built in to a camera which gives an indication, usually by signal lights, when the focus setting is correct.

Focusing, focus
Lenses are only capable in theory of focusing one plane sharply at a time. You can not have 2 metres and 6 metres focused simultaneously. In practice, normal lens apertures permit a general zone of sharpness in front of and behind a focused point. For best results, the most important part of the subject should be the point of perfect focus, set either by using the camera's focusing aids or on a distance scale.

Format
The size of film used, usually expressed as a number – 35mm, 110, 6 × 6, and so on – but in fact referring to the actual dimensions. 35mm has a 24 × 36mm format; 120 rollfilm can be 6 × 4.5cm, 6 × 6cm, 6 × 7cm or 6 × 9cm.

Frame
An individual exposure on film; a normal 35mm film has 36 frames on it. Frame numbers – the actual reference numbers pre-printed on the film, to help identify negatives or slides after processing. To frame a view – composing it through the viewfinder.

Hot Shoe
An accessory on the camera top which will accept a flashgun, and fire the flash without any need for an extra linking cable, as the contacts are built in to the shoe. Most current hot shoes also have 'dedicated flash' contacts which transmit control and exposure functions between flash and camera.

IR
Infra-Red. Infra-red light is used in many auto focusing and automatic flash systems. Photographs can also be taken by IR using special film and filters.

ISO
See Film Speed.

LCD
Liquid Crystal Display – a low power consumption, highly detailed information display which requires an external light source of separate illumination to be seen. Found on the exterior of electronic cameras, and also in viewfinders.

Lens Mount
The female socket, with a thread or bayonet action, which accepts a matching mount on the rear of interchangeable lenses. There are many different types of lens mount for the various makes of camera, and few are compatible.

Lens-cap
A clip-in or push-on cover to keep the camera lens protected when being carried or stored (do not confuse with lens hood).

Lens-hood, shade
A shade which attaches to the filter thread of a camera lens, to stop stray direct sun from interfering with the picture.

LED
Light emitting diode – self illuminating display for information, usually found in viewfinders. Can consist of lights only, or letters and numbers.

Macro
A general term for photography of small subjects needing very close focusing, and resulting in an image larger than half life-size on the film.

Manual
Separate setting of shutter, aperture or focusing with no automatic control by the camera.

Mirror lens, 'cat'
A special kind of very light, compact telephoto lens mainly suitable for wildlife and sports or news photography. Also termed a 'cat' from catadioptric, the technical term for the design.

Mode
Method or way in which a system operates – usually refers to choices by the user to select a different way of metering exposure, as in Shutter Priority Mode, Programmed Mode, Flash Mode, where a camera offers a range of alternative methods.

Monochrome
Black and white

Motor Drive
A motorized film advance system which operates at faster than two shots per second, or offers continuous shooting as long as the shutter remains pressed.

Negative
Film original with the tones and/or colours reversed, for making prints (not to be confused with slides).

Ni-Cads, dryfit cells
Rechargeable dry batteries, recommended for low long-term cost with flashguns. Nickel Cadmium cells, dry or gel lead-acid cells and other rechargeable types are available with various capacities and working life limits.

One-touch
A camera which can be operated with a single action or shutter release, performing all functions for exposure, focusing and film winding automatically.

OTF
Off the Film – referring to metering systems where the light is actually read from the surface of the film, during the exposure. Normally applies to flash exposure only.

Over-ride
Any control which locks or resets the automatic functions of a camera so that the user can change the result (e.g. full manual over-ride, factorial over-ride control etc).

Prism
Part of the viewing system of a single-lens reflex camera, which allows the focusing screen to be viewed in a right-way-round, right-way-up form.

Program shift
A function for changing the settings given by a programmed exposure camera, without altering the actual exposure. Changes a preselected shutter and aperture combination to a different one giving the same actual exposure (e.g. – 1/125 at f8 shifted using the control to 1/60 at f11).

Programmed, Program
Automatic exposure where the user does not have to set any controls, as both shutter and aperture are set by the camera. Some systems vary the programme to suit landscape, close-up or action (user selected) or the lens focal length (automatically set).

Rangefinder
An optical system which assists precise focusing using a simple form of triangulation, so that when two ghost images coincide exactly the focusing is set correctly. Autofocus systems use a form of electronic rangefinder.

Recycling
With electronic flash, the short period after taking a shot which the flash needs to charge up its capacitors before the next shot can be taken.

Remote Control
A means for firing the camera shutter without a connecting lead; normally radio, sonic or infra-red.

Reversal
Any process which results in a slide, or makes a print from a slide, rather than involving a negative.

Rewind
Most 35mm cameras need the film be rewound back into its cassette after the last exposure, by hand. Some do this automatically, with a motor; others wind the whole film out of the cassette before you start shooting, and it is rewound frame by frame so that when the film is finished the cassette can be removed without risk of forgetting to rewind. Other camera types do not require rewinding.

Self Timer (see Delayed Action)
A timing device in the camera which can be set to delay shutter release for a short period after pressing the shutter, e.g. 10 seconds, and allow the photographer to appear in the picture.

Shutter priority
See 'EE'

Shutter speed
The duration of exposure time – how long, in seconds or as a fraction of a second, the shutter is open to allow light to reach the film. As shutter speeds are normally fractions of a second, they are marked '125' for 1/125th of a second, '1000' for 1/1000th, and so on. Exposures longer than a second are written 1', 2', 4' (1, 2 and 4 seconds) in viewfinder displays.

Skylight
A camera filter with a very slight pink tint, which reduces a blue cast in colour pictures taken on dull days or when the sun is behind a cloud but the sky is generally blue.

Slide
Colour transparency, for projection, produced using colour reversal film.

Slow-speed warning
An audio signal in automatic cameras which tells the user to fit flash or use a tripod, because the shutter speed will be too long to hand hold without camera shake.

Stop-down preview
A device found on some single-lens reflexes which closes the lens aperture down from its full aperture focusing and viewing setting to the actual working f-stop set for the picture, to allow depth of field (focus) to be judged in the viewfinder.

Tele-converter, extender
An optional device which fits between the lens and camera and converts any given lens into a telephoto or long focus type. Normally doubles the focal length; 50mm becomes 100mm, 70–210mm zoom becomes 140–420mm zoom. Involves a reciprocal loss in light transmission; 2X converter, 2 stops light loss – 50mm f2 lens becomes 100mm f4.

Telephoto, long focus
Any angle of lens view narrower than 40° diagonally. On a 35mm SLR, any lens longer than 65mm focal length.

Tripod Bush
A threaded hole in the underside of a camera which allows it be fixed to a tripod or clamp.

TTL
Through the lens – normally referring to exposure metering carried out through the camera's own lens.

UV-Haze
A type of camera filter recommended to protect the glass of lenses in outdoor use; effectively clear, but also able to reduce excessive blueness in distant scenes and at high altitudes.

Viewfinder
The optical system you look through to aim the camera and compose the view which will be included in the final picture.

Wide-angle
Any angle of lens view wider than 50° diagonally. On a 35mm SLR, any lens shorter than 40mm focal length.

Wind-on, advance
The act of moving on to fresh film after each shot has been taken. Cameras may have 'auto-wind', 'thumb wind', a 'wind-on lever', or 'motorized advance'.

X, X-sync
The correct timing to ensure that electronic (rather than bulb) flash coincides with the full opening of the camera shutter. X-synch speed: the shutter speed at which this happens, normally 1/60 or 1/125. X-synch socket: a terminal on the camera for connecting electronic flash units.

Zoom
Any lens which has a variable angle of view, so that the scene covered can be altered without changing the camera viewpoint.

Index

Action photography, 38, 78–82
  equipment, 80–2
  planning, 78
  pre-focusing, 80
  viewpoints, 82
Aperture, 22, 26
  and depth of field, 27, 32–3, 106
  and exposure, 26, 32
  fixed, 22
  setting, 22, 26, 33
  variable, 22
Architecture, 86–9

Babies, 94–5
Backdrop, 134, 136
Bellows, 75–6
Black and white photography, 114–16
Bonfire, 103

Camera, 34, 35–9
  35mm, 35
  120 rollfilm, 35
  automatic, 21, 38–9
  instant, 35
  large format, 35
  one-touch, 35, 36, 37
  pocket, 35
  rangefinder, 35, 40
  reflex, 35
  single lens reflex, 23, 35, 38–9
  subminiature, 35
  twin-lens reflex, 35
  underwater, 91
  viewfinder, 35, 40
Camera shake, 77
Children, 94–5
Close-up photography, 75–7
  equipment, 75–7
Colour, 109–13
Composition, 57–61, 63–4

Darkroom, 142, 147
Depth of view, 27
  preview, 27
Differential focus, 24

Enlarger, 148, 149–52
Exposure, 22–33
Exposure controls, 29
  adjustments to, 31–2
  fully automatic, 29
  longtime, 99
  manual, 29
  multiple, 98
  selecting settings, 32
  semi-automatic, 29
Exposure meter, 22–33
  flash, 134
  types of, 29
  use of, 30–1
Extension tube, 75

f-number, 26
f-stop, 26
Film, 19
  and heat, 93
  choosing, 19, 21, 22, 108
  speed, 19, 22
  types of, 19
Filters, 52
  cross-screen, 52, 118
  diffusion, 125
  effects, 100
  for black and white photography, 52, 115
  for colour photography, 52, 125
  graduated, 52
  haze, 52
  polarizing, 52, 99, 100, 101, 107
  skylight, 52
  soft focus, 52, 101
  starburst, 52, 118
  ultraviolet, 52
Flash, 126–31
  bounce, 50–1, 95, 129
  computer, 127
  dedicated, 39, 50, 127–9
  direct, 135, 140
  electronic, 77, 80
  exposure, 130–1
  fill-in, 130
  infra-red, 84
  manual, 127
  remote sensor, 127, 129
  TTL, 50, 129
  twin tube, 129
  umbrella, 135
Flashgun, 39, 45, 50, 50–1, 77, 127, 129
Flowers, 105–8
Focusing, 25, 57
  auto, 38
  differential, 24
  on action, 80

Glamour, 66–9
  composition, 66–7
  lighting, 69
  posing, 67–8
  viewpoints, 67–8
Group photographs, 96–7

Interiors, 88–9

Lens, 14
Lens aperture, see Aperture
Lenses, 26–27, 36, 40, 40–9, 82, 122
  care of, 49
  catadioptric, 45
  choosing, 49
  close-up, 74, 75, 76–7
  fast, 26
  fish-eye, 82
  fixed, 40
  focal length of 26, 41–2

hoods for, 51
  macro, 46, 75, 76
  mirror, 47
  mirror telephoto, 45
  perspective control, 87–8
  portrait, 40, 41
  shift, 87–88
  tele converter, 47
  telephoto, 26, 27, 40–2, 44, 46–7, 78
  use of 48–9
  wide-angle, 26, 27, 40, 45–6, 78
  zoom, 40, 42–4
Light, 20, 102–4
Light meter, 21
Light trails, 103–4
Lighting,
  abroad, 92–3
  glamour, 66, 69
  indoor, 65, 117–18
  modelling, 133–4
  moonlight, 101
  night, 21, 102–4
  outdoor, 55
  photoflood, 140
  portrait, 63, 65
  still life, 71

Mattes, 100–1
Monochrome, 114–16
Moonlight, 101
Motor drive, 39, 81, 82, 83
  auto, 81
Multiple exposure, 98

Nude, 66–69
  composition, 66–7
  lighting, 69
  posing, 67–8
  viewpoints, 67–8

Open up, 26
Outdoor, 54, 55–61

Perspective, 87–8
Plants, 105–8
Portraits, 62–9
  candid, 62
  environmental, 62
  formal, 62
  informal, 62
Pre-focusing, 80, 83
Prismatic optics, 21, 100, 102
Processing, 142–53
  black and white film, 144, 151
  colour negative film, 145
  colour slide film, 146
  equipment for, 142–3
  in bulk, 153
  print finishing, 153

Red eye, 126
Reflector, 135, 136

Shutter, 22, 23
   automatic, 23
   speed, 19, 22, 23, 32, 80
Silhouette, 57
Slide copier, 76
Slides, 109–13
   viewing, 153
Small subjects, 85
Special effects, 98–101
Still life, 70–3
   composition, 70, 71
   equipment, 72
   lighting, 71
   subjects, 70, 71, 72
Stop-down, 26, 33

Studio, 133–40
   lighting equipment, 133–40
   lighting set-ups, 135–40
   requirements for, 134
Subjects, 11–12
Subject shake, 77
Sunsets, 121–5
Synchro-sun, 131

Television, 103
Theatre, 103
Travel, 90–3
   equipment, 90–2
   exposure and light, 92–3
   subjects, 91, 93
Tripod, 50, 51

Verticals, converging, 87
Viewfinder, 15–16
   attachment, 76

Water, 104
Weddings, 96–7
Wildlife, 83–5
Work, 117–19

X synchronisation, 128–9

Zoos, 83, 84